Kids Kids Kids

My Life Raising One Hundred Foster Children Over 30 Years

Marlene Burns

ISBN 978-0-692-78241-5

Contents

Dedication

Thanks to my loving husband Richard (also known as daddy), for one hundred and three children. I would not have been able to mother this crew without his cooperation for the 30 years it took to have those children.

Richard with first-born, Pamela

55 years later, with great-granddaughter Jilly

(still got that foot up)

To our daughters, Pamela, Michele, and Barbara, for sharing their home, bedrooms, parents, clothes, and vacations with our hundred extras. Thank you for helping to make our family special.

The Original Three Birth-Kids, Pam, Michele, and Barbara

Thanks to our daughter Michele for editing the book and formatting it to be "Kindle-friendly."

Thanks too to a special caseworker, Nellie Elsten, who appeared at our door so many times with more children to enrich our lives.

Forward

Marlene: Between 1965 and 1995, our family of two parents and three daughters grew to 103 children. We added newborns, and five pregnant teens, waiting to give their babies to adoptive families. Our oldest foster child was 19.

We had a mixture of boys and girls most of the time. Once there were eight girls and no boys, and another time there were six boys and no girls.

Our family activities included church, swimming, trips to the park, and YMCA sports. Nature was a central part of our lives, with hiking and camping in Indiana state parks, and many national parks. My job as an elementary teacher gave us fall, Christmas, and spring breaks, plus the whole summer to travel with the family, so we did! I believe people learn best by doing things, so we had our children doing things all the time.

Some foster kids were adopted by new families, others went back to biological parents, and a few went on to other foster families. Many kids were with us for three or four years, but one boy, Larry, stayed for keeps, eventually graduating from college, and giving us two handsome grandsons.

Note: Names and some details have been changed, for the privacy of the children, except where the former foster children have expressly given permission to use their real names.

The home of 103 kids- while we lived here

1 Introduction

In 1965 our Elwood High School principal, and the school nurse, were concerned about a sixteen-year-old high school senior wanting to graduate with her classmates. Her parents were divorcing and the girl's mother had full custody, but she was moving out of town. The principal and nurse were members of our church and knew our family well. Our five bedroom Victorian house was across from the school. They approached us about sharing our home with the girl, so she could graduate with her friends. We did have an empty bedroom, and our girls were ages three, seven and eight. We agreed to take her in. The local judge decreed the girl must go with the custodial parent. We never learned the girl's name and never saw the girl. End of the story? Not at all!

A Welfare caseworker heard that we said we would take in a child, and that led to our home being inspected, our children questioned, and my husband and I having criminal background checks. The girls were excited about sharing our house and having more sisters and brothers. We were issued a state license that said we could have one child from Child Protective Services. Our door was open! The first three or four foster children were "single placements," but eventually we were offered a group of siblings. I told the caseworker that we only had a license for one, but she assured me she could take care of that. The new license came in the mail and it stated we could have three children placed with us! In later years it changed again, to four, and then five. With our three biological daughters, our house filled up. I thank the Sullivans, Elwood High School Principal Blair Sullivan and School Nurse Lillian Sullivan, for setting us up for a very unique lifestyle. It all started because of their concern over one high school girl.

2 Pam

Our first foster placement was a girl named Pam, and our oldest daughter was also Pam. The neighbors also had a daughter Pam, who was around the house a lot. We solved the name problem by saying Big Pam, Little Pam, and Pammy. We later duplicated that solution with other names, Wendy, Richard, and David.

I explained to Welfare that we would not be able to take preschoolers during the school year, as I was a full time teacher. I would need to pay a babysitter for preschoolers, and my sitter would have charged more than we were paid by the county foster-care stipend. This meant that when the school year ended we got phone calls offering us children we couldn't take during the rest of the year. It was the little ones who made the family a lot of fun!

An example of that type of call came when Richard and I were planning our 25th wedding anniversary. We had grandparents taking our daughters, and "the fosters" were all being placed temporarily with other families. A phone call came and I explained that we were going to Alaska, and could not take a new child right then. I confirmed our trip date with the caseworker, but she said I would really like this one, and it would work for us and our trip date. She said he had been born that morning; I melted. I couldn't wait for Richard to get home from work. When he came in the door, I smiled big and said, "Hi, Daddy!" Still smiling I gave him a big hug and kiss and said, "You're a great daddy." He looked at me and said, "Welfare called, didn't they?" He added that he was going to Alaska without me. I still had my big smile and said, "You'll like this one, Daddy." He asked what is it and how old? I smiled more and said he was born this morning! We had only daughters, so this newborn boy was special.

There was a short pause. Richard said he guessed I could have that one. He realized most newborns are soon delivered to their adoptive parents, who have been waiting for some time, usually within a month of birth. That put the time-frame for our trip in the baby's schedule. We all enjoyed that baby for a month, and expected to take him to court on a Monday. This seemed like a good story up to that point.

Three days before the court date with the new parents, I got a phone call to get him ready on Saturday. I replied that court was on Monday, and we would be there. No, I was told, get him ready on Saturday; his mother has changed her mind. We were concerned. She had arranged for adoption because the baby's dad was her brother-in-law. Birth mother's rights trump, but her sister was mad at her, and her mother was mad at her; she would have no support system raising this child. Adding injury to insult, the sister's husband would be sending a portion of the family income away to support a child who represented the betrayal of a sister and husband. There was no chance for that baby to be in a family with his own mother and father, while a family, eager and ready for the child, anxiously awaited his arrival.

On Saturday we dressed him up cute, and his mother arrived at our home. She brought a cotton housedress to wrap him in. She had no money for formula, and no baby clothes or diapers for this wonderful baby. I sent all the formula I had bought, and left him in his little suit. As soon as she left I called the caseworker and explained the baby's new situation. They followed up and included parenting classes for this new mom. I cried a lot. It wasn't the ending I expected or thought best for him.

3 Ava

Ava came to live with us as our second placement from Welfare. She was 12 years old and from a large family of boys. She was a big sister to our three girls, now ages four, eight and nine. We worked with Ava throughout the school year but once the school year ended, it was decided by Welfare to place her in a group home where she would have counseling to help her. We were to let her adapt to the new placement and then they would allow us to visit her. The week before our visit could be scheduled, the new school year began. Ava and the other students living with her had their supplies in backpacks, and all their books. Off to school they all went. The other children reported her taking a detour. She never arrived at school. Her backpack and books were found in an alley, but there was no sign of the girl.

Nine months later, we had a call from California; Ava had been found living in a commune there. How she got there with no money was a mystery. They wanted us to take her back. Richard and I talked it over, but imagining what went on in the California communes, and what she had probably seen, we declined having her return to us because of the ages of our daughters. We didn't want her adventures in our house. Her next placement was the Indiana Girls School in Indianapolis. Years went by, and after her release at age 16, she became pregnant. She delivered a baby daughter in 1972. We got a phone call pleading, "Mom, come get this baby. I don't know what to do with her." We supported her and took the baby. Sometimes she would do OK, and other times she floundered, with poor people choices, no job, and just failure to "get her act together."

One day, we got a phone call from someone mumbling at us. I thought I recognized the tone of voice. I asked if this was Ava. The voice mumbled, "Uhha." She was in a hospital with her jaw wired shut. I asked where the baby was. She mumble-muttered an address and asked us to get her daughter. It was difficult to get all that information!

Upon reaching the location of the baby, I knocked on the door and a child about seven opened it. I saw four or five other younger children running about. There was a male asleep on the sofa, face to the back. No other adult seemed to be present. I asked the first girl where Tess was, and said I was her grandma and was picking her up. A child brought a filthy Tess to me. She had a dirty diaper on, her curls were matted, and that diaper was her only garment. The man on the sofa never turned over. Tess had been there for several days, following a bar brawl where Ava was badly injured.

I removed Tess and went to the Welfare office where they photographed her. They wanted to place her in a foster home, but I asked if I could take her for the weekend. I had her skin medicine and clothes for her at my house. I said I would bring her to the office on Monday.

It was very hard to turn her in, and I could have continued taking care of Tess, but felt that would have just enabled Ava to avoid being responsible for her daughter. Everyone involved in the bar fight had been drunk.

Welfare placed Tess with a family, but I did not know the location. A week later Ava was discharged from the hospital, still wired shut. When she learned we did not have Tess, Ava was very angry and made threats against our family and me. She said she knew people who would take us out! Welfare contacted my daughters' school and told them of the threats, and I was told not to go to my parking lot alone. Time passed and Ava was allowed to visit the baby. She began "getting her act together," and eventually met a nice young man. They married, and after counseling and parenting class, she was allowed to have Tess back. This man was not Tess's dad, but he adopted her and they were a stable family of three. We were again added to the babysitter list to care for Tess. Ava now realized we would turn her in If something was wrong in Tess's care.

Tess camped with us on weekends and in the summer. We were grandparents to her, a new title for us. She felt permanent when I stitched her name and birthdate on my wall sampler for my grandchildren. Ava cried when she saw that and declared total love for us. She appreciated all we had done for her, and for Tess. I still have a written note from Ava stating that if she was not able to care for Tess, Richard and I were to be Tess's parents.

Tess graduated from high school and moved to Florida and married a wonderful man. He owns a restaurant and supports the family. We went to their son's christening, and later, a daughter was also born to them. Tess has a good job and is doing all the things her mother never did. When Tess was about twenty-five, I delivered her baptismal certificate and dress, and lots of photos. All her trips with us and her history in her first quarter of a century were turned over to her to take care of. She will take care of it. Ava died at age 50. Tess is now an amazing, accomplished woman and mother. We are proud of her, and love her children too.

Grandma,

I want to start by saying that spending time with you and grandpa gave me some of the best childhood memories I have. Because you took my troubled mother in and stuck by her through the years, I was blessed to be your granddaughter, maybe not by blood but by what matters, love. You raised me when my mom couldn't. I spent holidays with you and best of all I learned some of my greatest life lessons from you. I learned to camp and explore. I have a strong love of reading because of you constantly sending us to the library. I learned that napping is a great thing, even though you don't want to.

Times were so different then. There was nothing like coming to your house and always being excited to see who I was going to get to spend my time with. There were always kids to play with and laugh with. We traveled everywhere and camped all over, spending time in the green van and playing games, and roasting marshmallows around a fire.

I loved Sunday school. I used to love going to school with you and learning about Indiana history. You were obviously my favorite teacher! I have so many memories, and as I write just glimpses now I have tears in my eyes because I cannot imagine what my life would have been like had you not taken in my mother and helped her through her teenage years, and even into her adulthood.

I wish that there were more people like you and grandpa to help young girls who, for whatever reason, have no homes of their own. I know that all the children you have touched have been blessed with love.

I love you! I am so proud of you for a writing a book. Like I told you on the phone, it's about time. You have so many wonderful things to contribute and you are truly inspiring, as apparently age has not caught up to you.

Tess

Tess Today

Michele here: Most kids came to us with nothing. I remember Ava had two ornamental bottles of perfume when she arrived, and she displayed them on her dresser like they were the crown jewels. She was very protective of those small possessions, which I respected. She liked me, however, so sometimes she invited me to smell her precious perfumes.

Ava was unlike anyone I had ever met. She seemed like a character from the movies. She was a firecracker, a fearless, brassy, street-wise kid, with a ready grin and no hesitation to speak her mind, to *anyone*. I was in awe of her. She did as she pleased. For example, Bobby Kennedy came through Elwood while campaigning for president in April 1968. Kennedy sat on the back of an open convertible and rode past the high school where, according to a news report, a thousand students lined the street to catch a glimpse of him. Ava did more than that though, she ran up and grabbed Bobby Kennedy's pant leg, for a "brush with greatness."

4 Baby Joy

The first summer newborn was a boy, but about a year later we got the call to come get a newborn girl. With the boy we had to wait a day for his circumcision, but with this little girl we took her home the day she was born. We called her Joy because she was a joy to have. We camped that weekend and she was in a front carrier on my chest. As we hiked the trails in the forest, people passing us would ask how old she was. On Friday I said she was born yesterday, on Saturday I said two days old. On Sunday I said three days old. Hikers shook their heads as I continued on down the trails. I didn't bother to explain how I got this child. If they didn't ask, I didn't tell how I was able to take trails up and down the hills so soon after her birth. Super Mom!

Shopping with her in the market was easy. She fit in the top section of my cart, where I usually put my purse. I was asked in every store how old she was. A store was the first stop after leaving the hospital because I needed formula. I kept a very straight face when I answered "She is five hours old." She was adopted when she was about a month old. We were told that if we heard of anyone adopting a new baby girl, we were not supposed to say anything. That made us think she was probably adopted in our hometown; a happy secret to have!

I discovered that *not* giving birth to a newborn child makes it so much easier to enjoy the child; there is no pain, no leaking milk, no physical discomfort of any kind. This baby truly was a joy to have!

5 Donna

One early placement from Welfare was a 16-year-old, pregnant high school girl. She came to Elwood "to babysit for me and help me out while I did my summer classes at Ball State University." She was my "live in" for the summer. That was the story her mother concocted for her dad and brothers. No one but her mother knew of her pregnancy. Her mom came to visit, but if she brought Donna's two younger brothers, Donna always sat on the couch with a throw over her lap. Her father never came to visit. Summer came to an end, and school was starting, but the baby wasn't born yet. Mom brought her school lessons for the week, and took back the completed lessons from the previous week. The school was told she would be late enrolling, as she had a severe asthmatic condition and could not be outdoors. Labor Day came and went. I started my fall semester at Ball State University, in Muncie, and our girls were in the elementary school in Elwood. Donna waited at home.

One Wednesday morning Pam came downstairs and said Donna needed me. I went upstairs and saw she was in labor. I called our doctor, took the girls to school, and Donna to the maternity ward of our local hospital. I figured she was in good hands, and I had class to attend in Muncie, 30 miles away. I told Donna I would be back as soon as class was over. I went straight to the hospital about 3 p.m. and asked for Donna. The nurse said she was not there; complications set in and they had to transfer her to Muncie! I had just come from there! I called my husband and told him what to do for supper, and where I was going and why.

I went back to Muncie to the maternity ward, and stayed there all evening and night. Donna stopped dilating, but her water broke. I went to my Thursday classes, and then back to the labor room. She was on antibiotics and they said there would be a dry birth. I called Richard and asked him to bring me a change of clothes. Friday morning there was still no baby. I went to class, and then back to the labor room. A surgeon came to explain that they would lose the baby and Donna without surgery. I explained about being the foster parent, and that I needed to call her mother. He said to do it immediately. I explained the situation to her mom and she told me to "Call me when it is over."

The surgeon asked why I was still there, and I explained Donna's mom's response about the surgery. I said I was not leaving Donna, as she was my daughter and I was responsible for her now. After the birth, I called Donna's mom about the baby girl, and she had a new story ready. Her husband and family were told that Donna had an emergency appendectomy!

Donna came home to our house a few days later, and her mom came to get all her belongings and take her recovered asthmatic/appendectomy daughter home. Dad and her brothers never learned about the birth. Donna finished her senior year and we attended her graduation. She met a nice young man and we attended their wedding a year later. She bore him a son and then twin daughters. These children were technically our first grandchildren! The babies were brought to our house regularly, and we followed their progress. Both girls were honored queens for Job's Daughters, and we attended their ceremonies. They graduated from high school as co-valedictorians and attended Indiana University, graduating with honors there. They both took teaching degrees, just like Grandma Burns!

Donna also took college classes and got her degree after the kids were raised. She claims us for her mom and dad, and the girls call us Grandpa and Grandma. We went to the weddings for both girls, and met their baby boys in later years. We are family!

My Life as a Foster Child

I was not the average foster child. I came from a very violent family, but a family who knew how to avoid anyone knowing how truly crazy we were. Then I made the mistake of doing what people in our social structure just DO NOT DO. I got pregnant, Christmas break of my junior year of high school.

The next few months were very difficult trying to hide things, vomiting constantly, and nowhere to turn. Then in my sixth month my mother figured it out. She took me to a doctor who confirmed. She demanded an abortion, but he said I was too far along. Between them they came up with a plan to put me into foster care, and to "get rid" of the problem.

We found out I could not be put in a foster home without my father's signature, so my mother's friend, a doctor, signed papers saying my father was mentally ill and could not sign. My mother tried beating me, but I remained pregnant. She had a friend who worked for the Department of Welfare, and plans were made to send me away. Family and friends were told I was going out of town to babysit. A friend of mine agreed to say he was the father, so he could sign the adoption papers, and the plan was complete. I was told to keep quiet and not say anything that would link back to my family. At this point I was still vomiting constantly.

I walked into the Burns home and right from the beginning I was welcomed, provided with maternity clothes, love, and support. The moment I felt the peace and quiet, the nausea stopped. No more middle of the night raids on my room, no more crazy outbursts. Just peace. Hard to explain.

Every visit from my mom was hell; constant lectures, constant wanting to know the real name of the father, and constant reinforcement of what a horrible person I was.

Then came time to go to the hospital, and the complications. Marlene held my hand, tried to coach, and tried to help. When she left me, my birth mother constantly said, "You are going to die, do you want to die with a lie? Isn't it enough that you are a whore?" The baby and I nearly did die and, to be honest, I wanted to. Marlene is all that gave me the will to keep going. The surgery for delivery, and the blood I needed put a problem in the master plan. To this day, when asked if I have my appendix, I smile and say I don't know. My "appendectomy" was our cover story.

I was married within a year, and have been married to the same man ever since. We enjoy being professional Santas every Christmas. I have a college degree, and am working on another, and I have spent my life helping others.

Once I was married, I separated from my biological family, except for a small period of time. My birth mother died and her final words were how much she hated me. No one knows the truth about my placement with the Burns family until now. Thanks for sharing my story Marlene and Richard. Thanks for teaching me how to be a real family.

Donna Dietz Plummer, July 11, 2016.

Michele here: I remember Donna well. She was a very kind and cheerful girl. From her disposition, you would never have known the trials Donna had, and was, enduring. My younger sister Barbara was Donna's favorite, and they spent many happy hours playing together.

Donna and her husband as Mr. and Mrs. Claus

6 Got Christianity? and "No Hands-Just Eyes"

One Sunday early in 1967, a woman in our church stopped me on the stairs and asked me how I could let all those people in my house. Confused, I asked "What people?"

"Why, all those children that are living with you."

I immediately replied, "How could I not?" The children cannot help what their parents have done, but Richard and I can help how the children live now. That lady was a decades old church member, but she didn't understand the scriptures telling us to do unto others what we would want them to do unto us. There was another time if she had listened, "If you do it unto the least of them, you have done it unto me"- Jesus.

Everyone knows you have to use all your eyes, including the ones in the back of your head, if there are toddlers about. I like pretty things around my house and have colored glass bottles and antiques to enjoy. I could move everything but I choose to educate the kids instead. My bay windows have glass figurines and a collection of ceramic cardinals. One day my two-year-old neighbor child was playing alone; then I couldn't see her anymore. I went toward the family room and heard a quiet little voice saying, "No hands, just eyes, no hands, just eyes."

This sweet child was standing by the cardinals and her hands were behind her back. She remembered what I usually said, but since I didn't say it, she was reminding herself about the no touch rule! She did listen! It had to be very hard on her because two of the cardinals are music boxes!

Richard with the “No hands, just eyes” neighbor girl

7 Twin Boys

My school secretary came to my classroom whenever I received a phone call. One Valentine's Day she came to the door and asked if I was expecting again. I answered, "Did you get a phone call?" She covered my classroom while I went to the office for the call. The caseworker told me she had seven-year-old twin boys for us. I only had one foster son with our three biological girls, so four plus the twins would fill the last two twin beds we had. When I got home from school the caseworker was there on the sofa, with the twins, but she also had their nine-year-old sister. She smiled at me and said, "I know you will find a place for Amelia, too!" I knew we did not have enough beds. I smiled back and said, "Of course." We all had dinner and then we went shopping for school clothes for the next day, and for beds to increase our sleeping capacity. That was the night we started stacking the kids, in bunk beds!

Amelia was wearing corduroy pants held together up both legs with safety pins. The three had coats that I wouldn't have considered for animal bedding. It took a complete wardrobe for each of them. Most kids that came to us had only the clothes on their backs. I went to school that Valentine's Day with four kids, and came home to seven. Now the house was really full!

By summer, the twins were coming up on their 8th birthday. I wanted them to have something to remember always. When the police had picked up the kids to transport them to the Children's Home, they had never ridden in a car before. The parents had no car and used a grocery cart to carry kids, do laundry, and get groceries. I made a call to the local airport. I asked them if they had a plane and pilot that could take twin eight-year-olds for a ride over our house, the school, and the public swimming pool and park where they played. A pilot volunteered to do that for me, and on their birthday the twins, Amelia, and our youngest daughter, Barbara, took their first airplane ride. I took photos of the Piper Cub taking off and landing, with happy faces smiling out at me! After the ride we went home to a figure eight cake made of two angel-food cakes on a cookie sheet. Friends and neighbors helped the boys celebrate being eight. (There was plenty of cake!) It was a day of new memories.

8 Chimney Sweep, and Drunk at School

Richard was in 3rd grade. A nine-year-old boy who had red scars on the bottoms of his feet where cigarettes had been used to discipline him. As I prepared his bed, he watched in amazement as I put on the mattress a bottom sheet, a top sheet, a light blanket, and a bedspread. He was dumbfounded! He had never seen anyone put all that bedding on a bed before. He said if you were cold, you wrapped in a blanket and laid on a mattress on the floor.

After I finished making the bed, I reached for the back of his jeans to see what size clothes I needed to get him. He said a lady at the Children's Home had given him his underwear, so he didn't need any more of that.

I explained he needed a week's worth and he would be changing his underwear every day.

When we ate pork chops for supper he held the meat in his mouth, not knowing how to chew solid meat. He identified an orange as a "ball," and we realized that he had no idea what a fresh orange was. The school found him "lacking in cognitive ability," but we realized he had simply never been exposed to what most people expect a nine-year-old to have experienced. He began learning many new things and we saw his abilities grow daily.

About eleven years after Richard left us, I was sitting in the kitchen grading papers. There was a knock on the back door, then it opened and a tall, sooty man walked in and said, "Hi, Mom!" The voice was a lower pitch, but I recognized Richard and hugged him, soot and all. He was working in our area and had to stop in. The soot was because he was a chimney sweep and fireplace maintenance man. He filled us in on his adult life, and said he still had the Smokey the Bear he had gotten for Christmas at our house. We asked him to keep in touch when he could. His sister was also placed with us, after he had left. She had a different last name, but she told us about him and we connected Susie and Richard.

Richard and our girls on Christmas morning

Michele here: I think what I heard about Richard was that he was one of six siblings, and when his mother left, his father couldn't cope, so he dropped his kids off at the orphanage.

I recall, with angst, quarreling with Richard once when we were out playing. I treated him like any other child my age, and when he upset me I lashed out, which was unusual for me. I felt a moment of elation; I had one-upped *a boy*! Then I saw Richard's face and felt awful. Looking back, I am even more horrified, because I was "real," while he was a foster child (vulnerable to being sent away.) I unwittingly put him in a terrible position. Add to that whatever abuse he had been through before, which cowed him, and it was inexcusably cruel. He has probably forgotten the incident, but I cannot.

I remember Richard's father came to see him once. He seemed a very sad man, but happlly bore a gift. It was a sort of troll dollhouse, I think, meant for a younger child than Richard, and just the house, nothing in it. The gesture, however, meant a great deal to Richard.

Later, another brother and sister pair came to us, Shane and Gabby. The girl was older, but the boy spoke for them both. She was in sixth grade, and he was in fifth.* We had the kids, but no formal paperwork came with them, so the next morning I delivered them to school, telling them what the boy had told us. When I got home from school I had an envelope from the school explaining that the children's previous school had informed them that our fifth grader was really a third grader, who unsuccessfully tried to promote himself!

Kids do try to be smart, and they like to think adults are not as smart as they are!

Shane the faux 5th* grader, Gabby, Larry, Tess, neighbor Jeananne, and niece Tish

Alcohol was available in our home, but only for New Year's, or special occasions. It was stored in a high cupboard, above the regular cupboards. None of our kids had ever bothered it, but Shane found it and was apparently taking a regular drink of whiskey before school. I left for my school a little before the children left for their schools. The children all knew what he was doing, but no one told us. One day Shane must have taken more than usual and his third grade teacher reported him to the principal as drunk. We got a letter and had a conference with the teacher and the principal. We had a talk with the boy, and all the kids who did not report him!

A month or so later the city had a conference for the parents from all three elementary schools in town. The principal from our school stood before that group of hundreds of parents and said he was so proud that there were no children in his school with drug or alcohol problems; I was dumbfounded! I knew very well about one child that had such a problem. How could he lie about that? If one boy could do it, and we knew that one, then there was a possibility that other children might be doing it too. The parents needed to be aware and watch for signs.

I almost wrote a letter to the editor of our newspaper telling that I knew about a third grade boy who did go to school drunk at that school, and the principal did not let the other parents know. Later I wished I had.

9 Curly Carl

One blond, curly headed two-year-old was all boy. He played with trucks, and wagons, and blocks. He loved to swing and go down the slides at the park. One day at home, he lined up dolls across the sofa. Boys played with dolls at our house and it does help boys practice to be good daddies someday. I wasn't watching too closely, but I had one ear open. He said baby cry, baby cry, over and over. Now I did watch closer. He got a throw pillow and put it on the face of one doll. He held it there and said baby no cry. I asked him what he was doing and he said this is the way to make a baby stop crying. He used his two-year-old speech, but that was the gist of what he was saying.

I reported these actions to his caseworker because his three-month-old baby sister was found dead when he was taken into custody. His parents moved to Ohio and, as far as I know, they were never charged with anything. We were told that no court would use a two-year-old as a witness. We felt sure he did not learn that by himself; he had seen a murder, as far as we were concerned.

He had the curliest head of blond hair and folks always thought he was a girl, so we took him to a barber and cut those curls. I saved them, the product of his first haircut, and gave them to his adoptive parents.

Years later I got a letter with a photograph inside. Carl had gotten married and had a baby daughter. The photo was of the baby at the same age as Carl when he was adopted. She looked like the same blond, curly headed child her daddy had been; cloned! We appreciated updates on our children over the years.

Curly Carl, Marlene, and Kenny,
getting acquainted with nature

10 Caseworkers and Wyeth

Our caseworkers were the most important contact between Welfare and the families of our kids. They supplied any information they thought was necessary. Sometimes I was called to court to testify on behalf of my children. I was always under oath for my statements. We had a new five-year-old son who was very skinny. He was the youngest of seven siblings. The two oldest were boys, ages ten and 12. Those big boys were caught stealing a six-pound box of hot dogs from a carnival vendor. The vendor had seen them steal it, followed them home, and called the police.

The police found the door of the house blocked, so they entered through a window. All seven children were home, but both parents were gone. Little furniture was in the house, beside the chest blocking the front door. Piles of clothes and blankets were all over the floor. The children said they slept on the piles. The police didn't find any food in the cupboards. There was a box of hot dogs in the refrigerator- nothing else.

At the hearing, the prosecutor called me to the stand and asked if I had a clothes washer. I said yes I did. He asked about a dryer and I said yes. He asked about dishwasher and, as I said yes, the caseworker spoke up, stating that Mrs. Burns was not on trial, and please change the questions. The prosecutor explained he was showing how my house had many advantages that a poor family would not have. How could we expect the children to do as well in their family home as they were doing in foster care? The caseworker spoke up again and stated that a foster care placement was intended to be better than the home from which children were removed; it is expected to show children what a house could be like. A Welfare lawyer spoke next, asking if the court was aware that father was employed at General Motors, as was the mother. The father also painted houses for a side income. Both lawyers and the judge were astonished at the financial disclosure. Their total income was much more than mine and Richard's.

Those parents were rarely home, and the children were always hungry. Both parents were alcoholics and gambling addicts. If the boys had not been caught stealing hot dogs, there is no telling how much longer the kids would have been left in those terrible circumstances. The judge terminated the parental rights.

So that's how we got our five-year-old Wyeth! He loved our kids, and since seven-year-old twin boys were also with us at that time, there was a lot of boy-play.

In September, Wyeth was chosen by an adoptive family across the state. The caseworker picked him up and delivered him. We had no updates for about two months, and then I was called, and asked to make a house call; the parents said they were having problems with Wyeth. I said I would be glad to go.

When I went in the door, I saw white carpet, a white sofa, and white chairs. Wyeth's bed had a pink ruffled spread, and matching curtains. There was a shoebox on the floor by the bed, and on the dresser was the post office bank, a GI Joe doll, and books we had sent with Wyeth. I asked about the shoebox and learned it had his McDonald's and Burger King toys in it. “Where are his other toys?” I asked. Well, they didn't want to spoil him so they were waiting until Christmas so the toys would be special! I asked about his schoolwork and art from school, but there was none to show me; they didn't keep that.

I gave mom some suggestions about toys for now, games they could use to play with him, and decorating his room with the school art that all kindergartners produce. When I got home I called Sears and asked if they delivered to a different address from the buyer's address, and they said “of course.” I ordered a cowboy and horses bedspread with matching drapes. I ordered magnets to put school papers on the refrigerator, and a set of Lincoln Logs to build with by himself. The parents agreed to buy a tricycle for now, and would add a wagon for Christmas. Now the house would look like a child was living there!

In March the parents called Welfare and said it was not working, and would they please come get Wyeth. I went with the caseworker and we worked out a story to tell him about why I had come that day.

I told Wyeth about a family that only had three little girls, and how they wanted a brother. The girls had a puppy and the puppy wanted a boy to take care of it! The puppy really needed Wyeth to take care of it. During the two-hour ride home, we convinced Wyeth that he would be perfect for the job. He finally said he would go to the puppy, since it needed him. This new placement worked.

There is a saying, to try, try again, and this time we had to do that.

My caseworker called to let me know that the first set of parents had filed papers to do another child adoption! Their request was denied by Madison County.

11 Four Beautiful Sisters

One of our biggest foster sibling groups had five sisters. We could only take four of the five; the youngest did not come to us due to our preschooler-babysitting problem. The sisters were ours for about three and a half years. They left, one by one, for adoption or other placements. They traveled with us in the summer, fall vacation, Christmas, and spring break. Florida was a favorite at Christmas, and Marco Island had a great beach and campground. All the girls loved those times.

Valerie was the fourth oldest and was chosen by a family with three sons, who wanted a daughter. Visitation went well and the family was enthusiastic about the new sister. Six months later we learned that the boys and dad were so loving, and lavished so much attention on her that the mother felt cheated, left out, and envious of Valerie; the marriage was in jeopardy. Welfare stepped in and removed Valerie from that family and put her immediately in a new one, but that ended when Valerie was molested by a family member. This little girl had been a vibrant, smiling, happy girl. My favorite photo of her was in the waves on Marco Island.

Valerie- Marco Island Florida, Christmas 1976

One day when the second oldest sister, Tracy, had been with us about a year, she snuggled on the couch with me and looked through my glasses. She exclaimed, "There are blue flowers on the light!" I looked at her and said they have always been on that light. She was an excellent student and we had no idea she was not seeing well. She went to the optometrist and she was fitted for glasses. Then her world was in better shape. I felt embarrassed for not realizing she needed eye help.

The flowered chandelier

Tracy, was selected for adoption after three years, and her response when we told her a “forever family” chose her was, "Why?" She didn't want to leave, but she did and they were an excellent family. Her new parents were a science professor and a pharmacist. Tracy’s new dad took a sabbatical to the island of Yap to study arachnids and Tracy got to live there for a year. When the family stopped in Hawaii on the way home, she bought us some Macadamia nuts, my favorite.

Tracy told her new parents about her favorite restaurant in Colorado, called Casa Bonita. It is a mock Spanish town, inside a restaurant, complete with a waterfall, cliff divers, jugglers, a story cave, strolling musicians, and a flag on each table to raise when you want to order more food, or get refills. They took her back there! It was a big hit with all our kids.

Tracy was a joy to travel with, and loved all we showed her, but her new parents opened up a bigger world. We attended her high school graduation, her college graduation from the University of Indianapolis, and later we went to her wedding.

While we met Tracy’s new extended family, one of our five-year-old foster girls went up to Tracy's grandma, lifted the glittering pendant she was wearing, and asked, "Are those real diamonds?" The lady was surprised and said, "Yes, they are." It alerted me that I needed to have a conversation about touching other people’s belongings, and not asking strangers very personal questions.

The oldest and the middle sisters both went to other foster homes. Tracy tried to keep in touch with all her scattered sisters. Later, we got to help with the oldest sister's wedding.

Barb, Marlene, Angie, Tracy, and Valerie in the Rockies

12 Kenny

Kenny was one of four children. He was 20 months old when he came to us. His parents had two older children, but lost custody of both of them, and the court system provided adoptive homes for them. Kenny was born and again the parents lost custody. Mom was pregnant with child four. Where was dad? He was incarcerated for raping a seven-year-old girl. After that, the court took Kenny's removal to foster care very seriously

Kenny was brought to us on Sunday afternoon. He was dressed in a diaper, and socks belonging to our caseworker's daughter. He was sound asleep so I just took him and placed him in the crib. When he awoke, I went to change his diaper and he began screaming and holding on around my neck. His private area was grossly swollen and red. I called the family physician and he said to be in his office in the morning. When he saw Kenny's privates, he looked at me and asked when the court hearing would be. He wanted to testify because he had never seen such a case of sexual abuse.

At the hearing Kenny's mom testified she did nothing wrong. She did what felt good for him and he liked it. I knew better. Gradually the screaming diaper changes quieted down. The presiding judge on the case saw that the couple had lost two children permanently, and decided that if they agreed to give up the baby she was carrying at birth, he would allow the parents to keep Kenny as their only child. They were to have parenting classes, and help in raising their son. While the decisions about Kenny's future were going on, we got a phone call. It was the father calling from jail! I didn't know prisoners had phone privileges. He had looked us up in the phone book and we were the only Burns family listed in Elwood, so it was easy for him. When he finished his sentence, he and his wife came to our house to thank us for taking care of their son. Kenny went with his parents, and the new baby was adopted at birth, and given a chance for a good future.

About a year later our caseworker called and told us the family was located in Arizona. They were sleeping under the alcove of a church. They had drinking water from the fountain and used toilets in the church. They were eating donuts from a local store that threw out the unsold products of each day. Someone reported them, and since Kenny was still on the county records of Madison County, the authorities in Arizona notified the authorities in Indiana. The little family of three was brought back to the Hoosier state, and services were again provided to the parents. We had hoped the parental rights might be terminated, and Kenny would go to a more stable family, but that didn't happen. Kenny was our youngest sexual abuse victim.

Camping with Carl and Kenny

13 Lori

Nine-year-old Lori came to us in time for supper, and we had a get acquainted time before bed. At bedtime, she announced she needed a light on and I showed her the moon was shining in her window. I said the sooner she shut her eyes, the faster morning and the new school would be here. I assured her I would stay right there beside her. The rest of the house was asleep, but an hour later she was still sitting at the headboard, definitely not asleep. I told her I needed to sleep to be able to teach the next day. At 3 a.m., she was still sitting by the headboard. At six, I got ready for school and fixed breakfast for the house. I left a call to the caseworker about the sleep problem. This is what I learned.

Neighbors who lived by her family saw her getting on and off the school bus, but never saw her playing outdoors. Mom was a stay at home mom. Dad owned and operated a car dealership. The neighbors thought it odd that the child was never seen outside. Months went by and they finally called the authorities. Welfare and the police went to the home and found the girl was being kept in her bedroom, where she had a mattress on the floor. No dresser or chest, but her clothes were folded on the floor at the end of the mattress. Her meals were served in that room, and she was to put the empty dishes by the door. She had a tin can for a toilet. The bedroom door was locked- on the outside. Knowing this made us try all the harder to help her get to sleep, and adapt to normal sleep habits. It took many weeks, but finally she would lay on the bed and pillow.

Fall break arrived and we were to go to our daughter's house in Virginia. We stopped at a motel en route, and all sleep gains disappeared; Lori sat at the headboard all night again. She did the same at my daughter's house. Once home in Indiana we began the adjustment process all over again.

At the end of the school year Lori was moved to Ohio, to a therapeutic group home with trained counselors. When school began I was taken to Ohio for her conferences. I was her parent of record. I didn't see her homework or know her teachers, but I was a parent! Eventually she was moved to Indianapolis, where visiting weekly was a nice change. She still needed advanced care and special housing. She looked like a pretty young girl, but she had major problems. That abuse by her parents had taken a terrible toll. It also took a toll on our family, and we cannot call her time with us a success. She got to see the Smokey Mountains, the Atlantic Ocean, and Colonial Williamsburg, but there was no peace in her heart. It is hard to know or understand how any parent could treat a child this way. Her case moved on and eventually we stopped getting information about her progress or location, but we hope she has found healing and happiness.

Michele here: I could always tell when foster kids had been loved, or not. Those who had known love had a kind of resilience. I could tell that a four-year-old I will call Phillip, had been well loved, and it broke my heart that his mother had lost her children.

Phillip's mother had four boys, ages four, three, two, and six months. Then her husband walked out. Overwhelmed, apparently, she left her kids alone at the house, sometimes, apparently, for days. Four-year-old Philip became the parent and kept his brothers alive. Eventually, crying alerted a neighbor who called Child Protective Services. My parents were given Phillip and the six month old. I have never seen a more protective and responsible four-year-old; he was like four, going on 25. He did everything for his brother, diapers, feeding, comforting, as tenderly and skillfully as an adult. My mom put the brothers to sleep in a bedroom off the living room, and then shut the bedroom door so the TV wouldn't disturb them. I was watching TV, and after my mom closed the door, Phillip got out of bed and opened it, five inches, then got back in bed. I quietly closed the door again, and he opened it again. This happened one more time, and then it hit me- his mother probably closed the bedroom door before disappearing. I left it open.

Back then, I found it unfathomable that a mother could walk out on her kids like that. Then I had three kids of my own, two years apart, and it suddenly made sense. I was never seriously tempted to follow her example, but I definitely understood it!

Philip and his brothers were eventually reunited with their mother. When I heard that she gave birth at sixteen, and had four children by nineteen, I felt sorry for her; if I had been in that position I may have needed to get away too! The mother was provided with services, she met all the requirements, and she got her children back. Success. I do not know about the father as the foster families were not in the loop in those days.

14 Sharon

Sharon was an early, single, foster daughter. She was nine or ten when she arrived. She was a willing helper for me, but if Richard put a hand on her shoulder or patted her back, she flinched. It took months to get her to realize a male could hug her or pat her on her back, and it was a "good touch;" nothing more would happen.

Our trip that summer was west: St. Louis, Kansas City, Dodge City, and into the western mountains. Swimming pools were a requirement for a campground en route. Our girls were like fish, but Sharon was timid about the water. She would go onto a diving board, bounce, then stop. Then she would repeat the attempt. One foot, bounce, stop. That happened in Kansas City, and again at each subsequent campground. I don't remember if she ever did actually dive into a pool.

We decided on a Dude Ranch with horse rides in Colorado. Our girls had ridden in the state parks in Indiana, but Sharon had never ridden a horse. She had been eyeing the steep hills around us, so I explained to her that in the mountains, the trails zigzagged, and you did not go straight up. When the girls were aboard their mounts, the trail boss started out and his trail literally went straight up that mountainside. All my talk was worth naught! They were on a 45 or more degree ascent starting the ride. Sharon turned around and looked back at me with a white face, but it was an enjoyable and successful ride in the end.

She climbed the cliffs into Cliff Palace at Mesa Verde, and went down into the kiva in Spruce Tree House. She listened to the naturalist tell of the ancient civilizations that had lived in the cliffs. In Yellowstone, she loved the fumaroles, geysers, and mud pots. In future trips in Indiana she got better at new adventures.

One day when she was 25, she called us and asked how we could afford those long vacations. She was a beautician, and was still single and struggling. She had figured out the value of travel.

Tired mountain hikers, taking a rest in the shade.
Barb, Richard, Marlene, Sharon, Michele

15 The Travel Bug

We traveled whenever possible to state parks, national parks, and more. Camping was the best way, and many national sites were free across the United States. Whoever lived with us, traveled with us. The Welfare caseworkers often commented that they wanted to be in our family. Before foster kids arrived, we had taken our daughters and Janet, the daughter of Richard's boss, to many state parks, and to Illinois, Kentucky, and Yellowstone National Park. All the state parks of Indiana were popular, from the Dunes, to Turkey Run, Spring Mill, and McCormick's Creek.

After the early experience of miserable rainy nights camping in a tent, we upgraded our nature accommodations by renting a tent camper for a week. Then we did two weeks. Then one Christmas, Richard received a shirt that had a flaw in the fabric. We took it back to Sears for a refund. There happened to be a travel trailer dealer across the street, and what fun it was to wander through all the new campers the first week in January.

The sales clerk was sure we needed to buy one. We told him all the cash we had on us was the five-dollar refund from the Christmas shirt. That wise dealer assured us that a five-dollar deposit was fine. He had a Wheel Camper pop-up that slept six. There were two double beds in the ends, and the dining table lowered to make another double bed. We decided that was a perfect $5 deal. Over the next thirty years, we went from the tent camper, to travel trailer, to a motor home. We went to Yellowstone 25 times, so that as many foster children as possible could see what was their very own property! The mountains, glaciers, rivers, lakes, geysers, and deserts are treasures belonging to all Americans.

The pop-up camper, Princess, and Michele's best friend Jill, at the Indiana Dunes

My brother and his family lived near the Indiana Dunes State Park. They all joined us for picnic dinners, and swimming in Lake Michigan. Uncle Richard made fantastic "drip castles" in sand, with new nieces and nephews.

Michele here: My mother's travel bug started when her parents took her traveling, domestically, as a child.

This is the car that allowed my mother's family to travel: a 1946 Nash. That is my mother's little brother Richard, mom, her dad- Theodore Roosevelt Herr, her grandfather- renowned naturalist George Ruegger, and her grandmother, Isadora Huddleston Ruegger.

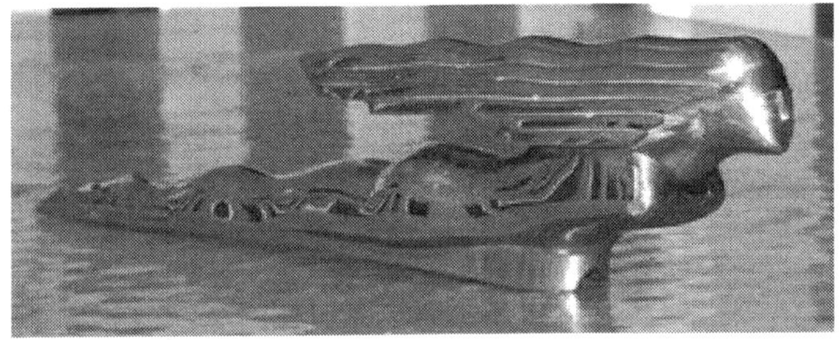

The hood ornament from the 1946 Nash
Photo courtesy of Bob Robinson

Mom says their first vacation in the car was to Yellowstone, back before there were interstate highways, and the roads inside Yellowstone were all dirt. They slept in the Nash, within spray-distance of Old Faithful. Mom's dad slept in the front seat; the rear seat pulled forward into the space where your feet would go, and the backrest laid down flat to make a bed, big enough for little brother Richard, her mother, and her Auntie Vi. Mom slept in the trunk.

Mom in the Badlands of South Dakota

My mother had more lofty travel ambitions, however, and set her sights on eventually visiting all seven continents. She and my dad checked off the last of the seven, by boarding a boat on the tip of South America. They sailed to Antarctica where they fell in love with penguins, saw the impacts of global warming up-close, swam in the hot caldera of a live Antarctic volcano, and watched their travel companions, a team of young Frenchmen, enter the Guinness Book of World Records as the first people to sailboard in Antarctica.

I think my dad also had the travel bug early. As a small-town boy from landlocked Indiana, he chose to join the U.S. Navy during the Korean War. He never got near Korea, but he sailed the Caribbean on a salvage ship, and saw a bit of the world outside of tiny Flora Indiana, though there were moments, I think, when he regretted it. He told me fresh fruit was a rare treat onboard, and on rough seas he once ate the same apple five times.

16 Remodeling, and Labor Day

We changed bedrooms around by age and gender all the time, but one room in our house needed major remodeling; our kitchen was too small. It was a typical 1893 kitchen, with a cast iron sink with a drain board, a glass-door cupboard by the chimney, and a 12-foot ceiling-not a modern area. Our contractor said he would begin renovating at the end of April. To cut costs, we all pitched in, taking out the doors, windows, and the south wall. We moved the stove and refrigerator to the living room, and the new lumber, and new doors and windows were moved into the family room. Then the phone rang.

The house was open to the world, and entry was by walking planks over the hole where the back porch had been. I explained we were in an awful mess, but the caller asked “Do you realize how badly these girls need a home?” I asked their ages, and my daughters heard me say, "18 month old twin girls." They began yelling, “Say yes mom, we'll help take care of them." We called friends to borrow cribs, since I only had one, and it already had a 14 month old in it. The dining table was in the empty kitchen, waiting for the contractor to begin the magic. The cribs straddled the lumber piles. When I checked one baby for a wet diaper, they all laid on the floor and wanted to be checked. We had a pregnant teen, and our three girls, so big girls each had a baby to mind. The eight females made for a crazy, but wonderfully exciting summer. Somehow, my husband survived it all!

Labor Day arrived and we set out to camp at Salamonie Reservoir, despite the condition of the unfinished kitchen. There are wonderful hiking trails, creeks to walk, and everyone loved the woods. On Monday morning, most folks took to the trails, but our very pregnant teen, Adelle, just walked around the campsite. About 11:00 a.m. she asked if wetness and blood meant anything. I knew she needed to return to the Elwood hospital. How fitting to have a girl in labor on Labor Day. I left Richard in charge of the other children, and arrived to check in on the maternity floor at 1:00. She delivered the baby by 3:00, and with her in good hands, I returned to the campground. Everyone figured it must have been a false labor, but I smiled and said, "It's a boy!"

Adelle came home a day later, and her mother was coming to pick her up. Before she left, she talked my girls out of the detasseling money they earned during July and August. Many teens did this job, detasseling corn, and it is the dirtiest, hottest, muddiest job ever. My washer should have been in a Tide commercial with the sox, jeans and long sleeve shirts that no one believed would ever be clean again. The girls gave her their entire summer's earnings, but didn't tell us. She told them, very convincingly, that she would pay them back. They wrote to her a couple weeks later, but never heard from her again. Now the girls had to tell us since they had no money for school clothes. It was a sad and expensive lesson the girls had, and it would be nine months before they could detassel again. The girls hadn't wanted Adelle to get in trouble, because she had been at the Indiana Girls' School before coming to us. Stealing would mean jail time, and they were protecting her from that, hoping she would be honest. She was family, after all.

The kitchen was finished by Halloween.

The new kitchen

17 Twins in the Bath

You know when the twin girls arrived, but now you can enjoy the odd developments after. They each had pink prescription medicine, but Violet and Viola had different last names. Their birth dates were the same! I called the pharmacy to be sure they really were to have the medicine. The pharmacist explained their mother had several last names and other children too. When he filled the twins' prescriptions, he didn't notice using two different last names.

That evening at bath time, I put the 14 month old in the tub, which was a regular treat for her. We had her from birth. Earlier, at diaper changes, there was a nasty diaper rash on both twins and I had coated their rashes with Vaseline. Now I was hoping a warm bath would be soothing. I undressed the first twin and leaned over the tub, but she grabbed me around the neck and began screaming. She just wouldn't let go. I tried several more times, but the screaming didn't let up. Finally, I set her on the sink, gently washed her, and got her in her pajamas. I tried the second twin and got more loud screams as I leaned over the tub. The 14 month old just played with the tub toys. Twin two got the sink treatment, and into her pajamas. The same thing happened on Monday and on Tuesday nights. Never had we had a child who did not want to play in the bathtub. Wednesday night came, and I got the 14 month old in her pajamas first, and then I got in the water myself. I had Richard hand me a twin. She sat on my lap and I put her toes in the water. I gradually moved my legs so she was actually sitting in the water and enjoying the tub toys. No tears or screams. I handed out twin one and took twin two and did the same treatment of toes first, then gradually into the water. No tears and no screams. Success! Thursday bath time was a breeze, and I didn't even get wet.

The next Sunday was visitation day for the parents of the twins. I told mom the severe diaper rash had healed, and the girls played well, and ate and slept well. I also explained I had a very hard time getting them into the bathtub, even with the 14 month old in there to play with. Mom started laughing. She said the girls had never had a bath before! I was dumbfounded that 18-month-old babies had never had baths. Mom said none of the houses they rented had ever had a tub. I was always learning from my children's experiences.

18 Homework

Homework was a nightly chore. Lesson plans, grading papers, report cards, and those were my jobs. The children all had lessons too. What I did not finish in the evening, I had to finish before breakfast. I made sure the children finished all their work at night.

Two 4th-graders could give each other their spelling words. No excuses about not having the list at home. They could also quiz each other in science and history. Mixed ages meant the older child could help the younger ones. It paid to have multiple kids, as everyone was good in at least one subject during homework time.

In the last year of our fostering, we had three girls in 5th grade, and two first grade boys. Do you remember how slow beginning readers actually read? I listened to them every night, and they were each assigned specific amounts of time. I do admit that I graded papers while they read, on occasion. The girls were able to quiz each other, but all written work was done individually. Having a teacher for a mom meant there would be no excuse for not completing lessons. I developed ways to get every assignment finished.

One "reward" I used was to let the girls grade my students' papers. This was a win-win. My teacher-helpers reinforced their own knowledge, and my workload was made smaller. My helpful fosters were allowed to go on my student field trips if they were age compatible. I did stretch that if our field trip was of great interest to a particular child, regardless of age.

My other "homework" was housework. Laundry had to be done, and even preschoolers could fold washcloths and match socks. Cooking was required, and the family was never sure too far in advance what was for supper. I often prepared two meals at the same time: one to eat, and the other for the next day, when I might already be prepping the next day's meals. It worked for me, but it took organization.

19 Conferences

School conferences are important tools to coordinate between families and school. I expected my pupils' parents to attend my conferences, and my own kids expected me to attend their conferences. One fall there was a new 3rd grade teacher at Edgewood, my kids' elementary school. She did not know me, or that I had taught at that school six years before. When she got her parent list to work out time for my 3rd-grader's conference, she made unflattering assumptions about me.

When I arrived in her classroom she was very cool to me, but asked me to be seated. She stated that Tracy was an "A" student, achieving well, and seemed very stable and secure, in spite of the way I lived my life. I was confused. I told her we always try to help our kids to be secure and stable, but what did she mean by "the way I live my life"?

"Oh," she replied, "with all the men you live with." I immediately said I only have one man in my life, and he has been there for over twenty years. She showed me the list she had to work with, to match a time with a 6th grader, B. Burns, a 5th grader, A. Rice, a 3rd grader Tracy, 2nd grader D. Akin, first grader V. Akin, and kindergartener W. Young. Six children with four different last names! She looked at me expectantly.

She listened to my explanation about being a foster parent, and was surprised the other teachers had omitted explaining the status of our family. I went home to tell Richard that I was accused of having many men in my life!

20 In the Newspaper

One year the Indianapolis News asked us for an interview for the upcoming Mother's Day edition. Our count of kids at that time was thirty-one. They thought it was worthy of an article. A photographer and reporter arrived and began photographing kids. The reporter was interviewing and taking notes. Kids sat on the organ bench and others stood behind them. I was in the background listening a little bit. It was the children's time to shine.

As I was listening to all the chatter, one voice came through very clear and loud. The voice said clearly that she was going to be adopted one of these days. I looked to be sure, but that voice was our own youngest daughter, Barbara! I said, “Sorry honey, you are stuck with us and cannot be adopted.” Barbara was born in the hospital hall, and we had talked about that birth many times. When the doctor arrived and saw the baby, he had said, "Got in a hurry, didn't you!" Barb knew some kids in our house did leave to go to a “forever home” with a new family, and I guess she wanted to try that. Every child crossing our doorstep was an equal family member.

What A Family — Just 31 Children

Richard, Marlene, Barbara, and four foster daughters

31 FOSTER CHILDREN - Mr. and Mrs. Richard Burns of Elwood have been foster parents to 31 children since 1967. They are shown here with five of the girls living with them two months ago. Mr. Burns is the son of Mrs. Marie Burns of Flora.

Burns are foster parents to 31 children

Mr. and Mrs. Richard Burns of Elwood have been foster parents to 31 children since they started in 1967. In addition they have three daughters of their own.

Burns, formerly of Flora, is the son of Mrs. Marie Burns of Flora. He is now employed at Pioneer Hi-Bred International, Inc. at Tipton.

Mrs. Burns, Marlene, a grade school teacher at Tipton all this time, has earned her master's degree since the first foster child arrived in the home.

The children have ranged in age from three months to 21 years. They include a set of boy and a set of girl twins. Five unwed mothers lived in the home until their babies were born.

While some of the children have returned to their actual parents, some have been adopted. The longest any child stayed in the Burns' home was three years.

The most foster children to be in the home at one time has been five. Those, coupled with the Burns' daughters, made it a houseful with eight children.

When the accompanying photo was taken with the five foster daughters, only one of the Burns' daughters, Barb, 16, was at home. One of their real daughters is now in Japan and the other is a college student.

The Burns family enjoys vacation trips. The children living in the home at the time always accompany them, where they go, including Florida, the Canadian Rockies, Colorado or anyplace else they travel.

Mr. and Mrs. Burns communicate regularly with several of the 31 they have helped, frequently with some of them.

They gave one of the foster daughters in marriage and are grandparents to a daughter of another foster daughter.

Although they have had a lot of fun and many great experiences throughout the past 11 years, Dick and Marlene both wonder a little when they consider their real daughter, Barb, thought she was one of the couple's foster children. It was several years before she learned she was not

Richard's hometown paper did a story too

21 The Burns Bank

Every one of our natural children borrowed money from us at some time in their lives. It must be in a child's genes to see $$$ in adults' eyes. Foster kids were just like the natural ones, and we felt like a bank. When children had moved on, somehow they always remembered our phone number if they were short of funds, for whatever reason. Most paid us back and were proud of taking responsibility for the repayment. Others still owe us today. We supplied a car payment, a winter gas bill, and numerous water and electric bills to stop turn-off orders. We made a mortgage payment, and even funded an Orlando vacation. There were many ten and twenty dollar loans, and most of them were repaid. One girl borrowed $400, but before she could pay it, she had to move to a different house and it required deposits on the utilities and a last month deposit. That was $500 more. That $900 never made it home. Another girl had moved to Georgia and called when she needed bail money for a boyfriend. We didn't get that back either. Richard says that financial aid is one of the bonding elements in our children's lives!

22 Extra Thanksgiving Guest

It was Thanksgiving weekend and my parents and brother had just arrived at our house. We had several fosters and the house was full. We were preparing all the goodies for the next day when the phone rang. I wrote down an address and said I would take care of it. Then I explained the call to Richard and my parents. A child had been left at a mobile home park a week before. His mom was in the hospital, and a part-time boyfriend had taken care of him so far. Now he wanted someone to come get the child.

My dad said, "You are not going are you?" I smiled and said, "Yes I am." I found the address and brought the boy home. The kids had a blanket-on-the-floor slumber party that night, and Tommy fit right in. He was our Thanksgiving guest, and Friday, and Saturday and Sunday. I called the caseworker and asked what I was to do about school; he was a first grader. She said to keep him, as his mother was still in the hospital.

I took him to my school Monday morning, and one of the teachers I carpooled with was a first grade teacher. I asked if she would take him to her room. He would fit there better than in my fourth grade classroom. She took him, happily, and we did not tell the principal we had an extra student. On Tuesday, I thought I needed to tell the principal there was a visiting first grade pupil, and that I did not know when he would be leaving. Teachers have to be flexible to meet many challenges, and my principal was understanding, because he knew of my unique situation; he was fine with our arrangement. Tommy stayed all that week, and on Saturday his mom came to collect him. He had done all his first grade work, just with a different teacher! He had made new family friends. He was a visitor only, not a foster child, so no funds were involved in his stay. He made us thankful to be able to care for him those two weeks. Once people knew about us, we had a few other cases like this. We never knew they were coming, never knew when they would leave, and never were reimbursed by the state for their care. We just enjoyed them while they were in our home. My dad agreed that Tommy was a nice little boy to have at Thanksgiving time.

23 Padre Island

Padre Island, Texas, made a trip for Christmas special. We had two foster boys, ages seven and nine, and two biological daughters with us one year. Everyone enjoyed the beautiful sandy beach where we camped. The naturalists had created a Christmas tree of sea grass, with hundreds of sand dollars and starfish as decorations. Richard and I relaxed in lawn chairs in front of our camper. The kids played in the surf and built sand castles. Other campers began to stop and visit with us, and ask about our fostering. That had never happened anywhere we had been. We did not advertise or mention fostering. Our kids were always "our" kids, foster or biological. We could not understand how the Padre Island campers knew.

Finally, I called the boys and asked them if they were talking to people on the beach. They said yes. The nine-year-old, Dusty, volunteered that when people asked if the younger boy, Larry, was his brother, he always said yes. That led to more questions, because Dusty was Caucasian, and Larry was clearly Asian, Korean, to be exact. Now the mystery of our fostering was in the open on Padre Island.

After leaving the Island on the car ferry, we went to New Orleans. The experience of the French Quarter, the cemetery with top-of-the-ground burials, and street musicians, was new to all the children. The colorful architecture made you turn your head all the time to see everything. That part of the vacation was most interesting to Richard and I, while the children thought the sands of Padre Island, and the dolphins racing the ferry on the way to the mainland was the best part of the trip.

A family near our hometown eventually adopted Dusty, and we were able to attend his high school graduation. He later went to college and studied culinary arts. He learned how to make the animal and plant carvings that make food look wonderful! He is now married and has a son and daughter, and is living in Ojai, California, where he owns a store.

24 Mississinewa and All the Bikes

Camping across the state or country is the best way to travel with a big family. It is the only way to have inexpensive entertainment and recreation. The kids loved it, and we took our bikes everywhere. Richard and I had 26 inch wheels, one with a baby carrier on the back. Big girls had 24 or 26-inchers, and younger ones had 20 inch bikes, some with training wheels. We hauled tricycles inside the camper, and big bikes were lashed to the back bumper when we drove. One weekend we were at Mississinewa Reservoir, where they have lovely smooth cement drives, good for biking, all through the campground.

I woke early one morning to voices outside my window. All the kids were asleep, and even Richard was not yet up. I unzipped the window a little more as the two voices were talking about all the bicycles and tricycles. An awning on the front of the camper sheltered all the bikes overnight.

I heard, "Just look at that. That is sinful!" My ears really perked up at that. "In this day and age, with all the contraceptives available, no one should have to have so many children!" A second voice agreed.

I didn't want to wake any of the children, but I really wanted to talk to the ladies and say, "Yes, we have seven children with us. I didn't give birth to any of them, and they aren't grandchildren either. They will learn about trees, flowers, and animals this weekend. The outdoors is the best nature center we can find for anyone's children."

This happened after all of our girls were grown and married. We continued fostering for a total of thirty years. The titles of Mom and Dad never wear out.

25 Yellowstone, Glacier, Hikers

Some of our favorite scenic nature spots are Bar Harbor Maine, The Florida Everglades, Glacier National Park, Mesa Verde, The Grand Tetons, Mammoth Cave, and Yosemite. We loved driving west and seeing the Arch appear as we approached St. Louis. Dad told the kids we had to drive over that big bridge to get across the Mississippi River. Our "other" kids went to all 48 lower states. Dad and I went to Alaska and Hawaii as anniversary trips, three times each. (No children went on those trips.) One Alaska trip was 72 days, a perfect vacation!

My extended birth family had reunions in Wisconsin, and my nuclear family was different each time we went. On one trip to Wisconsin and Michigan, we decided to go to Mackinaw Island. I was holding two boys, 18 and 20 months old. One was a blond, with curly hair, the other had straight, brown hair (Carl and Kenny.) An elderly gentleman was talking to them and making them smile. He said, "My, you sure don't look like your mommy!" (My hair is black.)

We traveled to the Rocky Mountains with various children, in different family groups. One year we visited Yellowstone and Glacier National Parks. Our daughter Barbara was with us, and three foster girls, Angie, and two sisters, Tracy and Valerie.

They were good animal spotters, and found elk, antelope, bison, bear, pica, mountain goats, and sheep. They swam in the hot springs, and waited for Old Faithful to erupt. Every evening we went to the naturalist-led fire pit talks. The girls straddled a huge log. Trees that large had to have been growing for centuries.

Our collection of girls watched a stagecoach robbery at Jackson Hole. The Snake River in Wyoming provided white water rafting on a hot summer day. An eagle swooped down behind us and plucked a fish out of the water with its talons. It made memories.

We headed north after Yellowstone, to Glacier National Park, and we saw a young couple walking along the road, wearing backpacks. They were hitchhiking, and we don't usually pick up hitchhikers, but this couple looked harmless so we offered them a ride. They were French, and the woman did not speak any English but the man did, so we were able to converse. She was a nurse, and the girls all had their pulse and blood pressure checked, with smiles! We hated to see the couple leave at the next waterfall trail. That was the only time we ever had a "resident nurse on board," to help occupy the children.

At the Athabasca Glacier, we hiked to the top edge and the girls sat on plastic and cardboard to slide down. Today, global warming is shrinking many glaciers. According to the USGS, there were close to 150 glaciers in the park when it was established, but a recent survey found only 25 large glaciers remaining in the park, and a computer model predicts that some of the largest will be gone by 2030. It is a great environmental loss.

26 Nightgowns

Our hometown had one large department store, Leeson's. The clerks knew me and sometimes they had good bargains I could use for my many children. One day a clerk asked if I could use some nightgowns for our girls. She had about two dozen gowns in all sizes, from toddler two, up to girl size 14-16. Most were white, but there were three or four pink ones. All were long sleeved and ankle length. There were embroidered rose buds and leaves across each bodice. The fabric was silky on the inside and fuzzy soft on the exterior. They were very beautiful! I happily told her any girl would love to have the gowns.

The clerk then explained why they were all available. The U.S. Government had just passed a new law requiring children's sleepwear to be non-flammable. The week before these gowns were on sale, and there was no problem. Now the fabric did not pass, and the nightgowns were to be destroyed. She said it would be up to me if I wanted to accept them, and I must realize they were not fireproof. At that time none of our clothes at home were fireproof! That was not an issue for buying clothes before the new law. The clerk knew about our girls and hated to see all the gowns in the trash, if they could be saved. They could not be sold, so those beautiful gowns went home with me. It was several years until all were given to new girls. Finally, one last white gown was left, size six.

Then came a phone call. A sibling group of three was on their way to our house. Two boys, ages seven and five, and a sister, age six. She would get the last nightgown. After supper and playtime, baths started and I put Nan in the tub. After she was washed and shampooed, I showed her the nightgown. Her eyes were shining and the smile was a big one! She petted the soft fabric. I told her it was hers, and she wanted to know if it was hers to take home when she left. I assured her it was totally hers to take. We slipped it over her head, and she grinned ear to ear and kept petting the outside. The boys finished their baths and we sat on the sofa for a bedtime story. Before we could go upstairs to tuck everyone in bed, Nan had an accident and didn't make it to the bathroom. She cried and was upset. I hugged her, cleaned her up, and put that new nightgown in the laundry. She had to wear a T-shirt to bed that night, but I promised the soft nightgown would be ready for bed the next night.

There were no smokers in our house and very little fire danger, so that was the basis for accepting $240 worth of nightgowns. I'm sure many stores across America were caught by the new requirements. Our house had fire extinguishers upstairs and downstairs, and in the front and back. We were grateful to get such fine items, and took care that we did not jeopardize the children. It helped our clothing budget, too!

Those three siblings were the first and only kids to camp in our new truck camper that fit in the bed of our pickup truck. We had a travel trailer that was our usual camping unit, but we bought the slide-in-unit to use on a trip to Alaska. We discovered, however, that two adults and three children taxed the confines of that truck camper. The weather was hot and sticky. We put the boys on the table bed and put Nan at the end of our queen size bed, above the cab of the truck. We went to Turkey Run State Park and hiked the trails and creeks. We all got dirty and sweaty. The shower house was busy with everyone trying to get cooled off.

Two adults might have been OK, but five bodies in that confined unit did not work. The kids had a great time in the woods, but we put a sign on the camper when we got home: For Sale. Bigger is definitely better in campers.

27 Three Boys

We had one family of three sons, ages four, seven, and nine, Zack, Chris, and Josh. Their mother was ill, and Child Welfare sent the boys to us. In those days, single fathers raising children was considered unorthodox. We met the grandparents and they were lovely people, but felt they were too old to care for the boys. Their mother was very creative and she made craft items that I used in my classroom. The boys' mom became more ill, and eventually died. Richard and I attended the funeral.

We took the two older boys to Yellowstone, and when you are in cowboy country you ride horses. We bought two tickets, but when the younger son got close to his horse, he realized how high up he had to sit. He wanted no part of getting on that tall animal! We couldn't even get him to ride a pony led around in a circle. The corral did not give refunds, so I took the ride in the mountains that day with the oldest son!

Those boys' dad never missed a visit day with his kids, nor was he ever late. He seemed an ideal parent. One fall he entered the chili cook off sponsored by *Red Gold* tomato cannery. His recipe won first place! The boys left foster care and, as I remember, they went to an aunt. Dad would sometimes stop by our house with them to say hi. I later saw his name in the obituary column and called to find out what had happened. He had skin cancer and it was discovered too late to save him. The three sons were all still in school, and were orphaned.

Years passed and we sold our 50-years home in Elwood, and while we were packing up we had a visit from the oldest son, Josh. He was a firefighter and had nice big muscles- just what we needed to get all the furniture down from the upstairs bedrooms. We could not have managed without him. His wedding was a week later and we took a present to them, met his beautiful bride, and shared a meal. They now have a handsome baby boy.

Josh, Chris, & Zack

28 The Four Brewers

Every trip with foster children is on record in photos. Each foster child was given a book of photos, complete with labels and story line. Each sibling had his or her own book, with self-portraits, as well as siblings, if they were with us. I never knew if the kids would be uniting with the biological parents, or with adoptive families, with or without their siblings. Every child was special.

One western trip was to Colorado, Utah, Nevada, Arizona and Wyoming. Four siblings meant four books to make. There were some duplicates, so each book had photos of the other kids. I no longer remember how long that family lived with us, but they had several years of vacation trips. Eventually the state returned all four to their mother. They had thick scenic records of America's natural heritage. I visited at Grandma's house several times, and they seemed to be doing well. Then one day when I went, and they reported that their photo albums were gone. I asked what happened, and they said Mom couldn't pay the rent and the landlord had emptied their apartment, taking everything to the dump while they were gone. I asked if any of them had taken a book to Grandma's house, but that hadn't happened; sadly, all was lost. I thought that the landlord had to realize what those books represented, and to just destroy them was wrong.

Four little "swimmers"

These two sisters and two brothers were fun. I asked if they could swim and they all said yes. The first afternoon out, we stopped early enough at a campground with a pool so the kids could swim while I fixed supper. Turned out, *none* of the kids could swim! I started with them one at a time, blowing bubbles, face in the water, holding the edge of the pool and floating, and finally I held each body as they really did float. At the end of that month-long trip, all four really *could* swim, thanks to daily lessons.

Circus-Circus was a hit as a casino, but also as a show venue. The children got to see performers their own ages doing fantastic gymnastics. They were also, for good or ill, introduced to gambling. All four stood on the tile floor at the edge of the carpeted casino floor, because children were not allowed on the carpeted area with the slot machines. Richard sat at the closest machine and deposited nickels to the cheers of his fans. The coins clicked down, and the cheers were louder! Money was won- enough to buy double dip ice cream cones for everyone. I hoped we weren't setting anyone up for gambling problems; ice cream, after all, is a mighty good association! After Reno and Las Vegas, we headed east to Wendover, Nevada. It is located on the Nevada-Utah border, and gambling is legal in Nevada, but not Utah, so it was a crowded campground that night.

A gorgeous, giant motor-home pulled into the site beside us. The driver got out a step-ladder and began cleaning the huge windshield. My cherubs sat on our picnic table and watched, with great interest. I was also impressed. The children asked questions and the neighbor answered. When the coach was clean, he invited the children to come see the inside, but he said they had to pay a quarter for a ticket. Jack was the only one with a quarter, so the man reached into his pocket and gave quarters to the other three. They went into the motor home for a tour, and I wished I was with them; million dollar campers are not what we were used to. Smiling faces came back out, along with bowls of popcorn and soft drinks. The wife directed them to the picnic table. That family was not only generous, but they were wise about where children should be eating! I thanked the man and woman for being great entertainers.

That night the kids all had showers and went to bed. Then I took my turn at the shower house. As I came out the shower house door, I heard shouting from across the campground. The kids were shouting at me. "We won, Mom, we won!" As I got closer, I signaled them to be quiet. I told them we could be asked to leave, for disturbing the peace. What did they mean by we won? "We won money, Mom! Our quarters won, and Mr. Perdue brought our winning money to us." Each child held a roll of coins! The neighbors, the Perdues, were good Samaritans! Later I talked to them and said they had no idea of the imprint they had made on these children.

We learned our neighbor had been an administrative assistant to Mr. Henry Ford, and was retired from Ford Motor Company. The couple traveled in this vehicle to where they wanted, and when it was time to go home they left it in storage. They flew home to Michigan, and when they wanted another trip they had someone move the vehicle to where they needed it next. What a way to go!

Our kids wrote post cards from all destinations, and then brought them home, saving postage. On longer trips, we did send a few in the mail. Communication was set up with foster children's families before the trips, so the kids could call on particular days and times. We didn't ever know where we actually would be, so we had to call home to the families. I remember, sadly, that this family never did receive a call from their kids, because they were never home for those appointments.

29 Disney with Five Boys

Over time, people have asked us which is easier, boys or girls. We had eight girls at one point, and six boys at once, and I can quickly say that of those two groups, the girls were much easier to manage. That particular group of boys were 16, 12, 12, ten, eight, and four. The older three were singles, and the younger three were siblings, the Baugh boys. We decided to take them all to Disney World and Cape Canaveral for spring break. We learned there would be a bonus at the cape, because there would be a launch while we were there. The sixteen-year-old opted to stay in Indiana, as he had been to Disney a couple times. I agreed and made the arrangements because it made more room in our vehicle for the others.

We camped at the Disney campground and began touring the Magic Kingdom. Jimmy, a 12-year-old, complained about the rides. Why do we have to go on those? This is boring. I don't like all this music. The other 12-year-old, Chet, joined in the moan and groan tirade. Those two boys were a major complaint department. The three younger boys were having a ball. At midday, Richard took the four-year-old to the camper for naptime, while I continued on in the Magic Kingdom, reaching as many attractions as possible. Next, we went to Epcot. The hanging back, muttering, and hateful comments didn't stop. I began to wish we had not invested in this venue. All our previous children had loved this "Happiest Place on Earth!" But not my two twelve-year-olds.

At last, we reached the "Hall of Presidents." As luck would have it, the doors closed right in front of us. We would be the first in to be seated for the next presentation. More complaints and muttering. I faced the boys and told them they were going inside. They were going to sit quietly so all the other Disney visitors would be able to hear. They could shut their eyes, and not look or watch anything going on. But, they were not to talk and spoil any visitor's time at Epcot.

The presentation began and President Lincoln stood up and made his speech. I felt a nudge and a whisper in my ear said, "Mom, I know why you brought us here. All the kids in your class would like to be here. I like this!" I smiled because Disney got through to at least one of my twelve-year-olds!

We went to Cape Canaveral next. It was special to me as I was in the "Teacher in Space Program." There, I had cooperation from four of the five boys. The last twelve-year-old was not giving up. The boys saw the huge rockets, the space shuttle, astronauts, and a giant movie screen. Reality hit the boys hard when they saw a film shot from space about the Blue Planet. Hearing the thrust of the engines and feeling the vibrations and the rumble in their seats during lift-off finally made a difference for the last 12-year-old. He said it was "neat!" Success at last! After we left the movie, four-year-old Zach fell and skinned his knee. A passing astronaut picked him up, and by luck I caught it on film.

That trip was the most difficult of all the trips we had ever taken. I was glad it was spring break, and only nine days long.

30 Jimmy

Jimmy was a normal looking boy, with dark hair and eyes. He seemed to have many relatives but, nonetheless, was placed in foster care. We were not given any information about his family. Christmas means gifts, and our foster kids received very little from relatives, but Jimmy was different. He received more than all the other kids put together. Boy toys, games, puzzles, clothes, and more. I thought he would be happy to have so many siblings to play all his new games with him; games usually need two or more players. Not Jimmy.

For a few days, when someone asked to play with him he just said no, and then shut the door to his bedroom. He was so possessive of his games and toys, he refused everyone. In mid-January, he took every one of the new Christmas games apart and piled the pieces in the middle of his bedroom floor. He tore down the curtains from the window and put them on the pile. He had a box cutter (that I didn't know he had), and began slashing all the puzzles, games and curtains. There was a floor-to-ceiling bookcase in his room, and he slashed the spines of every book on every shelf. All his beautiful new Christmas presents were ruined.

I reported to the caseworker, describing his anger. They set up counseling sessions for six weeks. We took him, waited for the half-hour time to be up, and then asked about the session. He had refused to talk to the counselor. He even refused to say his name. They tried questions, and waiting for an answer, and tried just waiting for him to volunteer anything. Nothing came from him. He remained mute the whole six weeks. The useless sessions were discontinued. When he was transferred from our home, we had no idea where he was placed. We hoped it was somewhere where they knew how to reach a very troubled boy. He did have a nice smile, but it was very hard to get to see it.

Seven years later we saw Jimmy working at a Taco Bell; at least we knew he was still alive. We wondered about his temper and anger problems. We hoped they were resolved. This was the boy who went to Disney World and could not be happy in the "Happiest Place on Earth."

31 Wendi in Plimoth

One summer we traveled east to Maine, with Bar Harbor and Acadia National Park as goals. We had two daughters by birth, and two foster daughters with us. Highlights included visiting a doll museum at Mystic Seaport, Connecticut, and the four girls found that a natural place to be. When we entered, a docent asked us to sign the guest book. It happened that we used the last lines on the page and the docent turned to a fresh double page. Our four-year-old, Wendi, had not yet signed and she asked to do so. The docent looked at me and asked if she could write her name, and I verified that she could. The docent handed Wendi the pen. Wendi took it and wrote WENDI, from the top of the page to the bottom, across both pages! The docent hid her mouth behind her hand, with her eyebrows lifted high. I can still see her expression today.

Going south from Maine, we stopped at Plimoth Rock, and the Plimoth Plantation Village. They enact life in the 1700s, and speak and answer in the speech of that period. One woman was mixing something in a bowl and, of course, Wendi asked what she was making. The woman said it was a cake. The four-year-old could only think of one kind of cake, birthday cake! She asked the pioneer presenter if it was a birthday cake, and the woman said she had never heard of such a cake. Immediately Wendi began describing birthday cake, and told the woman how to mix and bake it, and how to decorate it, including the candles. The period presenter could hardly keep a straight face. Our little encyclopedia was sharing her broad knowledge.

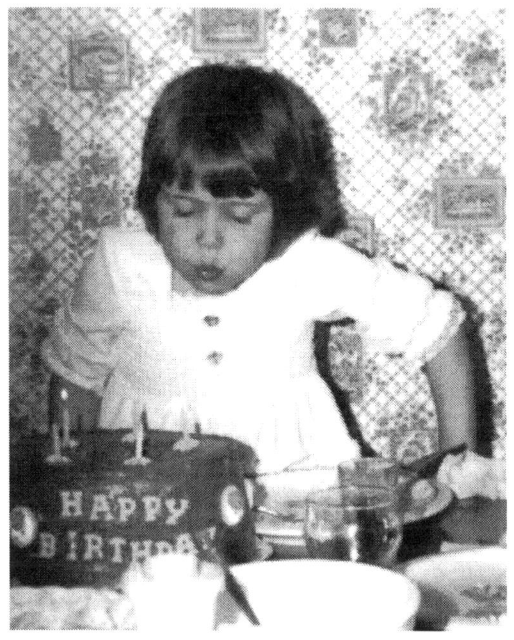

Wendi- Cake Expert

Back at an amusement park in Indiana, we were riding a train around the grounds. Wendi, never a shy or quiet child, sat across from an elderly man and she asked him if he had brushed his teeth. He was startled, but after a pause he said no, he had not. Wendi began at once to give him tips for good brushing, including how often he should do it, and even how to rinse. As we were getting off the train, he quietly said to me that he didn't want to lie to her, so he said he didn't brush, but he actually had dentures and he soaked them. These lessons came from a special little girl who asked me if I was “perturbed” with her if she thought she was doing something wrong!

Wendi and Angie

32 Wendi at Riley, and After

Wendi went with my class on a field trip when she was five. My fourth graders were mostly nine, but she fit right in with them with her interest in the Indian dancers, the pioneer exhibits, and huge canoes on the Wabash River. She loved the fry bread, the story tipi, and all the beautiful costumes. My principal and superintendent were my bus drivers that day. They fell in love with my "windy Wendi." She didn't know a stranger, and was loving to all.

Wendi was having headaches often. They were very severe, and the doctors at Riley Children's Hospital had diagnosed her with migraines, but said it was very rare to happen at her age. One doctor at Riley took a personal interest in the child, when she realized Wendi was a foster child and her parents' rights had been terminated; Wendi was free to be adopted. The doctor and her husband did not have any children. The couple went through the adoption procedures, and she and her husband made the required appointment to meet Wendi for a visit- a precursor to finalize adopting her.

Early in February, on a Sunday morning, Wendi fell out of bed and crawled over to my bed and under my blankets, saying "Mommy, my head hurts." I didn't realize it then, but those were her last words. We got up, wrapped her in an afghan, and went to our local hospital. They called an ambulance, and Richard went home to the other children while I went in the ambulance with Wendi to Riley in Indianapolis. That trip is much faster when you have flashing lights.

She was in the intensive care unit and visitors were limited, but I was allowed to stay with her full time. They told me to talk to her and exercise her arms and legs. They drilled her cranium to release the pressure on her brain. I asked her to make her eyes look at mommy. She did, and I called a nurse and she repeated it for the nurse. It gave me hope. She could hear and understand me. They told me when she said she had a headache, she *really* did, because of the cranial pressure. That day was the day her adoptive parents were coming to take her for a visit. Richard let them know she was at Riley. Welfare told us to contact her biological parents, because of her condition; they needed to know about their daughter.

Wendi's mom and her new boyfriend came. Dad and his new wife came. They were only allowed to visit for the 15-minute limit in the ICU. Four days later Wendi really became an angel.

I went shopping for a pretty dress and found an ankle length white one with daisy flowers all over it. The clerk explained it was the first of the new Easter season, and it was washable and permanent press. I couldn't talk, as I thought that it would never be laundered. I took the dress to our florist and asked for a headband of matching flowers, such as a flower girl would wear in a wedding. They matched her dress perfectly.

We had her funeral and our minister gave her eulogy. He knew Wendi from church and did a wonderful service, including all four sets of parents: foster parents, adoptive parents and the biological mom with boyfriend and dad and new wife. My principal said he had never heard a service so fitting for a special little girl.

After the autopsy, we learned that Wendi had a herniated brainstem. It is a birth defect, and no one realized Wendi had it. Most babies born with a herniated brainstem will die before their first birthday. She was five years old. A kindergarten classmate said kindergarteners don't die. I agree, and feel she lives on in heaven, talking her way into everyone's heart.

A week or so after the funeral I could not sleep. About midnight I decided to talk to God. I got a pen and paper and began my letter. I knew I wouldn't need to mail it as He would be watching while I wrote:

Dear God,

Yes, she is windy! What insight at the birth of a child to give her a name she so aptly fulfilled! Has she told you about the waterfalls in the Poconos, or about the coal powered steamship at Mystic Seaport? She couldn't wait to board the ship, listen to the wailing whistle, and feel the chugging surge of power as we left the dock. As she played with the antique toys in the old home in Mystic, she lovingly tucked the porcelain doll under its quilt. The docent raised her eyebrows as Wendi signed her name in the guest register in six-inch tall letters.

She loved the sands and ocean on Cape Cod. A flea market woman gave her a feather and piece of ribbon to put on a doll dress when we got home. You should have seen her model the fancy hats and jackets of days gone by, as only a five-year-old can. She was beautiful!

At Plimoth, she learned that pioneer children didn't have birthday cakes, and she told the lady there that it was a custom they needed to adopt. She watched the butter churning, petted sheep, fed hogs, and sat in the stocks. Ask her and she will explain all of that to you. She will probably tell you the people there say they are pilgrims, but she knows they are just acting that way. Oh yes, another ship she can tell about is the Mayflower. At first, the wax pilgrims onboard confused her, but she can explain that now too.

Ask her about the motor boat at Bar Harbor. She watched the lobsters in the pens, but didn't like the taste of lobster later. She listened to the Acadia ranger as he told about the Glaciers scraping across the rocks we climbed. She watched the Blue Nose Ferry going to Nova Scotia through the fog. We sat and watched the lighthouse blinking its light on and off. We listened to the buoy bells ringing their warnings. She will tell you about the ferry that had lots of cars on it, but had room for our camper too, as we crossed Lake Champlain. She watched the French voyageurs on the Wabash River in their 30-foot canoes. She loved visiting her sister in Dallas, Texas. Lord, she has probably bent your ears with tales from home. How many five-year-olds have led cheers? Her favorite is

"Eight bits, ten bits, two bit's a dollar, all for Elwood stand up and holler." She even performed that with IV tubes in her arms, standing in the hospital hall. She picked out her husband, a high school junior, but told him he had to wait since she was only in kindergarten. The yearbook staff had special crayons and paper for Wendi. As the high school kids made their page layouts, Wendi designed her own yearbook.

She didn't appreciate a Sunday School friend who said her name was Wendi because she talked so much. She decided to be Cindy instead, so if she tells you that is her name, now you will understand why. Lord, she is a special little girl. Her memory will astound you as she fills in details of her short life. She did a lot of living and helped those around her see the world with love, and matter-of-fact honesty.

She will give your "Littlest Angel" a run for his title. Her leotards always developed a tiny hole at the knee, which somehow grew to saucer size by the end of the day. I found bite size pieces of chicken in the pantry when a clean plate happened too fast. The coffee table wears a shade of pink nail polish on the bottom shelf. She pointed out more spots that I missed, behind some books. How I treasure each memory. She was a good spoon and beater licker during baking, and she was learning how to get an egg out of the shell for cookies.

Her kindergarten teacher explained that her group was an active and talky group, but Wendi led the way. She sang songs for the Christmas program at church. Her favorite is "O Come Little Children to Bethlehem's Stall." Ask, and you will know how it goes.

Lord, our minister says we are all yours and only share one another for a short period of time. Then we come back to you. I really do thank you for sharing Wendi. We tried to give her the care she needed. Thank you for entrusting her to us. She gave so much love to all she met. You trusted us with her and now we trust you with her. Her life with you can go on being eventful!

Lord, I have a favor to ask of you. Wendi was going to sit way back on the sofa so she could hold her sister's new baby. The baby isn't born yet, but if you have a little one there, please let Wendi hold it; I know she will be very careful.

Oh yes, one last word for you Lord, Wendi loves to go rock-a-bye and be held.

Then I slept well.

Michele here: Wendi was indeed a prodigious (and adorable) talker. Words just tumbled out of the child like she couldn't get them out fast enough. I remember thinking when she died, that maybe she knew her time was short, and she was trying to say everything she could before she left.

Marlene and Wendi

33 Smiths

Disney was popular as a destination more than once. I had vowed that I would never ride Space Mountain, ever again, but once there an adult had to be with certain short sized children, I found myself riding it one more time. This summertime trip had our blood grandson fitting in with a family of two sisters and one little brother. The oldest girl had wavy blond hair, and the younger girl had braids past her waist. Epcot Center had a venue, with a troupe of international dancers performing. Part of their presentation was to choose audience members to participate. A very tall African dancer chose our smiling seven-year-old, who was most willing. As he led her up the steps to the stage, the audience gave out an audible "Ahhhh!" She did every step he did, and kept in time with him. She gave a great Disney performance and loved being in the public eye.

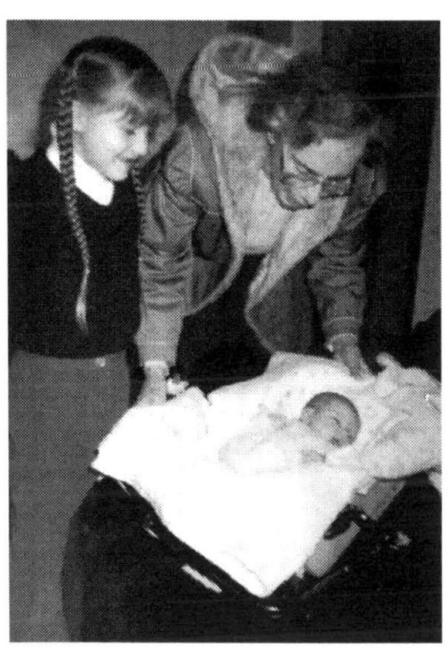

1986, Grandma Irene Herr with seven-year-old Disney dancer, and newborn great-granddaughter Lisa

The sisters stayed with us on into the school year, but the little brother was preschool and went, instead, to live with a county judge and his wife. They had dealt with the legal side of child cases over the years, and now were becoming foster parents with the intention of adopting this adorable young man. The boy announced to friends or anyone who would listen, that his daddy was a judge! The best-laid plans, however, can go awry. All three children were returned to their mother. Even a judge doesn't always get the last word, though the boy lived with him for quite a long time.

Marlene and mother, Pearl Irene Ruegger Herr

My mother moved into our home during the time those sisters were living with us, and she loved being their grandma. She waited eagerly for them to get home from school so she could help with homework. She carried their photos in her wallet. They were her family, too. We took Mom to Wisconsin for a reunion with her seven brothers and sisters. Our fosters were also a hit with my aunts and uncles. We stopped for a picnic supper at Tahquamenon Falls, in Michigan. None of the children had ever seen so much water spilling down. There was a logging museum nearby, and Paul Bunyan greeted us. Both the waterfall and the lumberman were giants! Naturally, this family added some great photos to their albums.

34 Cassie

Cassie came to us at age 11. She had reported to her P.E. teacher that her dad was molesting her. Charges were filed, and she was removed from her family. She was an angry, combative girl, and she often argued with other kids. She didn't work well in our family. That summer I asked Welfare if a different placement was better for her. I tried everything, but her emotional issues were severe, and she would not cooperate. Another home was arranged for her in Fort Wayne, and I had to deliver her to the Bronnenberg Children's Home in Anderson as a way station to her new foster family. As I was taking her to the home, she kept saying she was going to jump out and run away. At my wit's end, I said she would be in a lot of pain from falling out of a moving vehicle, and I managed to get her there in one piece.

The Fort Wayne family tried their best, but there was no working with her there either. She was returned to Bronnenberg, where she stayed until her 16th birthday. She was then returned to her biological home, and her dad was finally put in jail. She did not accuse other family members, so no charges were ever filed against them, but others, we learned, had molested her as early as age six. Her family remained angry with her for making the charge against her dad.

At age 18, Cassie gave birth to a daughter, Emily, who had a congenital heart defect. Guess where she brought the new baby? Back she came to us. I held that tiny child, watching her chest raise and lower slowly. Her skin was very blue. I kept thinking, don't die, please breathe, breathe and don't die in my arms. Emily had open-heart surgery when she was a month old; her incisions went from sternum to spine, on both sides. We later called those her zippers. As Emily grew, Cassie left her with us often. It wasn't an official foster placement, just a kindness on our part. I asked Cassie to let Welfare legally place her, so we could receive funds for her food. Cassie refused, saying she would never let Welfare have her daughter, even if it would help her get on her feet.

We continued giving help to that blue baby, and took her to Riley Children's Hospital for cardiologist appointments. Because of her heart condition, she was not expected to live to adulthood. We always made sure she had the heart medications that were keeping her alive. At age ten, little Emily, in effect, became a mom, when her mother gave birth to daughter two. Emily did all the childcare for the new baby. Mom slept a lot, and did no housework, laundry, or cooking. Emily did the night care and fell asleep in school because of Sandy, the new baby. Cassie later rented a house a few doors down the street from ours. One day Emily came to me asking for a baby bottle. I went with her to see why she needed it, and counted 28 dirty baby bottles around the house. Some were even in the sink. Clothes were knee deep all over. Seventeen months later, Cassie gave birth to daughter number three, Marcy. When Cassie went into labor, I kept the two older girls, and Richard took Cassie to the hospital. We asked Cassie to get her tubes tied, and she agreed, but the hospital didn't do it. We made sure there was an appointment later to get that accomplished. Richard took her to the hospital for the appointment, and we felt relieved that it would be the end of Cassie having more fatherless babies (the father of the younger two was already married, with children in another state.)

Cassie's two younger daughters grew, and both of them went on their 8th grade trips to Washington DC. We told them we would do the same for them, as we had for Emily.

We sent six kids on that DC trip. I remember the first one costing $105, and the last one was $750. Inflation! A foster daughter named Nancy was the last child we promised that trip to.

Cassie's girls traveled with us to the East coast, the Smokey Mountains, and Florida.

One night, Richard got a call to go to a local tavern to pick up Cassie at 3:00 a.m. Another time I saw her car behind the same tavern, where she liked to play the slot machines for money. I checked, and the three girls were in the car, alone. I left a note, took the girls home, fed them, and put them to bed. Later, the local police arrested Cassie and she was incarcerated, so we took the girls until Cassie could be home to care for them. The poor parenting events multiplied. Cassie always said she loved her girls, and we're sure she did, but there was no common sense about physically taking care of the girls. Emily's heart medicine was one thing we felt strongly that we had to get for her when mom didn't.

Mom Cassie was our real foster daughter, and her three daughters never went into the Welfare system, but I think they should have. Their situation was terrible. I reported that she needed help, and Cassie got a warning when a home inspection would be, and she still didn't pass it. They gave her another month and told her when to expect them, and she failed the inspection again. Reluctant to take her children, they gave her yet another chance. We were enablers because we cared about the three girls, and knew they needed us. We never had a penny of financial help, but we were repaid in buckets of love from those granddaughters.

As the years passed, we did what all grandparents do- we took care of those three girls. We were mom and dad for Cassie, and grandma to her girls. They traveled just as our formal foster kids did. Emily went solo with us to

Yellowstone, saw Mount Rushmore, and climbed through Mesa Verde. The little girls were too small at that time. We sent Emily on her 8th grade trip to Washington DC, and four years later we hosted a graduation party when the girl who was not expected to live got her high school diploma. In 2016 she turned 25. Many times I doubted that she would survive.

The girls all went to church from the earliest days they were with us. One of Sandy's proudest times was when she was old enough to be acolyte. It took a long time for her to be tall enough to reach the candles! After we moved to Florida, the First Presbyterian Church in Elwood adopted the girls for their Christmas project. They bought jackets, boots, mittens, and things like shampoo and toothpaste, along with school supplies and toys. Those lovely church ladies took over the job we had been doing for years!

Cassie's kids had photo books covering twenty five years, and I kept them at my house. All the girls loved looking at the photos and remembering their travels. They could also see what they looked like as babies. I had documented the first bike ride, first tooth lost, a dog bite in the face, the Easter bunny cakes, the first day of school for each, special programs at school for them, and they had the photos of their participation in the Elwood Glass Festival Parade. When Emily was studying U.S. history and they talked about national parks, she asked to take her book to class so her friends could see where she had been. The girls all did a trip with us to Missouri, and Silver Dollar

City. The cave located there was their first trip into our earth. None of the trips would have ever been possible with their mother. When Richard and I retired to Florida, the books went home to the family; it was their turn to take care of their history.

Michele here: Cassie illustrates the failure of family and society to care for a vulnerable child. I don't have all the answers, but here is an example of the problem. Cassie was abused as a child, and as an adult she makes poor choices and struggles. Her emotional issues or other deficits make it hard for her to keep jobs, or care properly for her kids. I remember once she got a dog and it had puppies. Over a couple weeks all the puppies died; I suspect she forgot to feed or give water to the mother dog, who was kept outdoors in summer. This illustrates the negligence her children experienced. When Cassie's daughter Emily came of age, she wanted to move out of her mother's house. They had a terrible row because Cassie was living off Emily's disability check (Emily is on disability due to her heart condition.)

One possible solution for people like Cassie is a guaranteed basic income, which might alleviate much suffering for those who, due to various deficits, lack the opportunity or ability to be regularly employed. This novel concept is gaining favor in many circles today. Guardianship of at-risk adults may also play a role.

Such people are everywhere, a small, but persistent percentage of the population. I see them in my job as an educator at a community college. I know families who struggle, trying to pool resources to support adult relatives who don't function well independently. I have students who may never hold a living wage job due to learning disorders, mental illness, or other issues that make them difficult to employ. Families are not always available to support these people, and I am convinced that we must have a robust safety net to keep them off the streets, away from crime, and to protect them from human trafficking or other abuses.

The challenge for society is finding the balance point between doing nothing, which some conservatives advocate, ("Survival of the fittest! Let the orphans starve."), and taking humane action to address the needs of this population, while encouraging and enabling whatever capabilities exist. I envision a program to subsidize jobs (not just Goodwill), which could offer meaningful experience and interaction, an opportunity to contribute, and self-esteem. Being proactive will save society money in the end, as we keep vulnerable people from harming themselves, or victimizing others, and out of jails, emergency rooms, and avoid other expensive, short-term, reactionary responses.

The fact that child protection services and foster care systems exist is testament to society's good intentions, but I know we can do better. Too many people still slip through the cracks, and we all pay that price, whether we see it or not.

35 Theatre Events

Our kids received regular education, religion, geography experience, and social skills. We picked out the best church clothes, and polished our table manners. We tried to expand their cultural experiences, for example, and took some little girls to see the live stage play, "Annie." It was performed at the Beef and Boards Dinner Theater, in Indianapolis. The girls ate, listened, and loved seeing all the live actors, especially Sandy the dog.

The next summer we took our experienced theatergoers to see "High School Musical," and they were thrilled again.

Our third year of live theater performances moved to a larger venue. The show was Cirque du Soleil! That super entertainment was so expensive we only went once with children. I wished there had been coupon savings for special places like Disney and Cirque, and I sure asked, but was refused, so we paid regular prices. I felt certain Disney would want to accommodate our foster boys, but I was refused, even after showing their credentials. They said large groups can order ahead for group discounts, but families are not big enough. Seeing the looks on the girls' faces, however, was worth the price! I loved it so much I was sorry Richard was left at home when I took the girls, so I took him a couple of years later for our anniversary (he was just as appreciative as the girls!)

36 Larry

Larry, and his younger sister Charlotte, were taken to the Bronnenberg Children's Home, and we were called to come pick him up. He was six and had just finished kindergarten. Charlotte was preschool, and went to live with another family in Elwood. I told Larry I was taking him home, where Dad was waiting, and we would have supper. He stated that he didn't have a dad, and then he told me I was ugly. I assured him he would have a dad at our house, and I couldn't help if he didn't like the way I looked! With that beginning, we started home and he became our longest time foster child. He traveled all over the U.S. with us. From his kindergarten beginning, he completed grade school, middle school, high school, and then graduated from Ball State University with a Bachelor of Science degree. His story alone would make a book. I am sharing only a few tidbits of his growing up.

The first thing I noticed about him when he smiled was that he needed a dentist. He had 20 deciduous teeth, and 22 cavities. The treatment meant many fillings, and seven extractions. It was the worst mouth of all our kids. Today he has fine teeth, and they are all his own. Larry's mother was from Korea and his dad was an American soldier. He looks Asian, and he and Charlotte were probably the only Asians in the small town of Elwood at that time. Their dad disappeared after Charlotte was born, and mom was trying to raise the two children by herself.

Mom worked, but the money was not sufficient, and she had alcohol problems. Welfare stepped in and we got a son.

One weekend Larry and his sister had visitation with their mom. While at his mom's, a fire started in the kitchen. Mom was passed out, and Larry could not put it out, but he spotted a passing police car and ran down the middle of the street, waving his arms to get the officers' attention. They saw him and called the fire department. Larry saved his mom, his sister, and himself.

Larry went on all our camping trips, and his sister came regularly. She made trips to the Grand Canyon, Colorado, Wyoming, and Montana with her brother. She also took a Christmas vacation to Florida one year. A private trip for both of them was to the Knoxville World's Fair, in 1982. There was a large Korean exhibit and we felt the children were old enough to have some Korean heritage in their education. They ate Korean food, heard traditional music, and saw photos of their mother's birthplace.

One of my favorite trips with Larry was to Missouri and the Lake of the Ozarks. While there, a pontoon plane landed on the lake and began giving rides. I love to fly, and Larry had not yet had his first flight (that he remembered.) I decided he should have a flight, and I had never been in a pontoon plane, so we climbed aboard. The water was a bit rough, and we taxied and taxied, up and down the lake, but were still on the water. I began to think I had purchased a bumpy boat ride! Another lap, and more speed, and we finally took off. Larry got his flight, with great views of the Ozarks, and I added a new form of transportation to my bucket list.

When he was in 8th grade, Larry was recruited for adoption by a couple that had already adopted an Asian daughter. They thought the two kids would be company for each other. That did not work out, however, and after two months, Welfare asked if we would take Larry back. We said, of course. He did not want to be adopted, and asked to stay permanently with us. The state agreed to the arrangement and he became our son. He ended 8th grade with one of the Washington DC trips.

Larry's high school Spanish class made trips to Mexico. His trips were to Cancun and Acapulco. Larry was on the high school Spell Bowl team, and played trumpet in the band from middle school through high school. He played at church for the hymns with fanfare introductions. He also played Taps at funerals. He was very proud of his concert trumpet.

In his senior year, he applied to work at a local grocery store as a stock boy. He was notified by phone that he had a job, and since they required black pants and white shirts for the job, we shopped and his jeans were left in the closet. He proudly reported for his first day of work, and an hour later he came home. He said they told him he didn't have a job. I asked him to watch the kids and I went to that store. I went to the manager's office and asked why my son did not have a job after we were told he was hired. The manager asked, “What is his name?” Then she looked at me and asked, "Is he *your* son?" She suggested he get a job out of town. I explained he was a senior trying to make funds for college next year, and he didn't need to drive out of town. After returning home, a stock-boy friend of Larry called and told him that he heard the manager say they wouldn't hire no Jap to take jobs from Elwood kids. I was MAD! He was not Japanese (as if that mattered), and he had lived in Elwood from age six. They refused to hire him. I should have pressed discrimination charges, but felt at that time it probably wouldn't have done any good, and feared it might even be detrimental.

We also had racist graffiti sprayed on the back of our garage, aimed at Larry. When that happened we tried to get it off and repainted before Larry saw it. Charlotte also met discrimination in Elwood, a town of around 12,000, which had once been a stronghold of the KKK. Ignorance and prejudice die hard.

While at Ball State, Larry worked in the computer lab. One day another student approached him and they realized they had the same last name. Larry said it would be funny if they were related. It turned out they were distant relatives. Larry began using the lab to find relatives, and located an aunt! She knew where the long lost dad was living. He was in Tennessee and had married a new wife. (He must have forgotten he still had a wife and two children in Indiana.) His new wife gave him two sons, then about ten and six- Larry's half-brothers. His aunt invited him to come to her home, and said she would take him to see his father.

Larry knocked on his father's door and when his dad opened it, said, "Hi, I'm your son." There had been no contact since shortly after Charlotte was born. Welfare had tried to find his dad, and there had been no Social Security number activity for him, so they presumed he was dead.

Then dad disappeared again, abandoning his new, illegal family. After Larry graduated from college, his father decided to get in touch with him. Today they communicate, and Larry took his sons to visit their real Grandpa, because Larry wants it that way.

Today Larry has a successful career in computer work, and has come a long way from that little boy without a father. Thank goodness we were chosen to be his foster family, even though he called me ugly!

Larry

Michele here: I remember when Larry came. He was a slight child, and his baby teeth were little brown stumps. There was a dentist a block away and my mom had a standing arrangement; whenever someone didn't show up for an appointment, the receptionist would call. If mom was available she would trot down the alley with Larry, and the dentist would pull a tooth. The dentist was afraid that the decayed baby teeth might affect the adult teeth underneath. That went on for a long time. It must have seemed like torture to a six-year-old.

Larry's mother came to visit him once, and brought a brown paper bag full of candy bars. The teeth suddenly made sense- she clearly didn't understand the link between sugar and tooth decay. (I think my mother made all that candy discreetly disappear.)

I was scared of what Larry would grow up to be, because of what he had been through in his early years. Today, however, I am happy to report that he is an exceptional father, generous, attentive, patient, and gentle; his kids are lucky.

Larry with his sons, Milo and Kirk

37 Mika

A special opportunity came about when Larry was in high school. We were full of fosters, as usual- five if I remember right. Our neighbors were accepted as a host family for a young student from Japan. Mika arrived and made friends in Elwood. The school year began and Mika was in band with Larry. She met all our foster children. Then the father in Mika's sponsor family, was transferred by his company to Japan, and his wife and baby were going with him. We suggested that Mika could cross the street and live with us. That seemed better than uprooting her successful start to her senior year of education in the U.S. The exchange program agreed to the placement and she was ours. What a wonderful addition she was to our family.

She went to football games, school programs, the prom, and graduation. She camped, and went to church with us, even though she was not Christian. She loved being big sister to the little fosters. They, in turn, idolized her, and loved to read to her. She instructed them in origami. They did holidays together, especially decorating for Christmas. It was a wonderful year.

Mika and two foster boys

A couple years later, Mika returned to America and brought her sister, Yuki, to see where she had lived. They explored together and found English schoolbooks to take home to Japan, to use for teaching English to children. They watched and helped make glass objects with Joe Rice, master art-glass maker, and heir to the famous St. Clair Glass Factory. The girls added beautiful glass objects to take home in their suitcases. They visited the local Ray Noble tomato-canning factory, to watch the processing of tomatoes, and cans of tomato products went into their suitcases. I lent the girls a large duffle bag to put their clothes in, which freed their luggage for all the souvenirs. The souvenir idea was a great way to show their family what was available in our little town. The glass items were gifts from the very generous Mr. Rice. After he helped the girls make the glass pieces, the glass had to be fired, so the girls visited other friends from Mika's school year. At last they were packed and on their way to Japan.

Marlene, Graduate Mika, Richard, & Larry

Yuki, Mika, and Richard, in the Elwood kitchen

One little snag occurred because of the generous gifts the sisters were delivering. The airline charged a generous fine for being overweight! Books, glass, and cans are heavy!

38 Angie

Angie was the oldest of three children, and her two younger brothers were also placed in foster care, with other families. She was in 5th grade, and participated in Girl Scouts along with our foster daughter Tracy. All our children went to church on Sunday, and participated in the summer Bible School sessions. When Angie was 12, she participated in the communicant's class for church membership, and joined the Elwood Presbyterian Church. In junior high, she became a Panther Band trumpet player, and was so proud to wear her Panther uniform. She was still with us in 8th grade, so she also went to Washington DC, and received the wide photo of America's Capitol, with her class in front of the famous building.

Angie traveled from Maine to the Rocky Mountains, and south to Florida. More time with us meant more travel. She experienced all the state parks of Indiana, and the Indiana Dunes and Spring Mill were her favorites. Turkey Run and McCormick's Creek were a close second. She bubbled over with enthusiastic love for our family. I once made her an Easter dress, and she so appreciated it, and everything we did for her.

At the end of eighth grade, Angie was of age to choose where she wanted to live. She decided to return to her biological parents. She had a grandmother she was very fond of. Welfare approved the move, and she moved about thirty miles from us.

Back with her parents, she dropped out of school, (not an option ever in my house), and became pregnant. Now she was a teen mom, and we got a phone call one day. She talked a long time, and said she was a bad girl. She kept that little boy and married his father. I do not know the particulars, but her husband was incarcerated for a couple years. After he came home, they had two daughters. The couple brought the three children to visit us, and we were grandparents to Angie's kids.

When the girls were school age she came to me and asked what to teach them, and where could she get books. I told her to please send them to public school and let them socialize with other children, so they would have a rounded education. Her husband did not want them in public school, and insisted that home schooling was better. I suggested she work with the local school, and they would guide her on what to use, with the appropriate materials for the ages of the children. That never happened, to my knowledge, and the girls were illiterate.

Angie told me she wished she had stayed at our house. She felt she would not have made major errors in judgment that were changing her life. She still visited occasionally over the years, and we supported her when she needed help. We brought household items, for example, to help set up a new apartment. Both her son and older daughter married.

Disaster struck, and Angie was incarcerated, along with multiple family members. She did nothing, and that was the problem. She didn't report any problems when her son in law was abusing her step granddaughter by feeding her salt when she "misbehaved." Angie's charge was neglecting to report anything suspicious. Angie's step-granddaughter became ill, and later died. Angie didn't know why. Her youngest daughter also served time, but was released after 18 months. The police asked Angie why she didn't report anything, and she said she didn't know to do it, or to whom she might have reported.

Angie is incarcerated still, and takes all the educational classes possible, which will reduce the time to her release. She has depended on her Bible, and on prayers from friends. She writes to me monthly. I sent stamps but they were returned to me. That is not allowed! I made an Easter basket woven of yarn, and blew out an Easter egg and painted it for her. I mailed it, and after she received it and opened the package, they took it away and put it in the trash. This has been a very hard time for her, but she is looking forward to restarting her life. She has grandchildren, she has faith, and she has love for others. We love her. Raising children is difficult in the best of situations, and this has taxed the feelings of all of us.

Dear Mom and Dad,

Being loved for the first time is the best. Camping and vacations across the country from the east coast to Canada's Rockies are my favorites. I loved Canada. You gave me the courage to be what I wanted to be. You accepted me, even when I made the worst mistakes of my life you were behind me. You never gave up on me. You're the best parents a girl could ever want or need. Dad gave me my first job, at detasseling corn. Mom, you gave me extra teaching. I can't forget the horrible trumpet practice coming from upstairs! But, I marched with the band! I loved the cooked Cheerios that Dad made. Oh how I loved all the holiday meals with lots of family, that I had never had. I loved horseback riding in Yellowstone. I am proud of myself now. I have my GED and work and life skills. I never accomplished much before. For those that said I wouldn't amount to anything, I am here, standing tall with family and friends behind me pushing me forward.

Love, Angie
(Summer 2016)

Angie and Valerie at Yellowstone

39 Pets

You might think that all we collected was kids, but we also had pets. We found a puppy abandoned in the woodland garbage dump at McCormick's Creek State Park. Then we realized there was a whole litter of puppies. Someone had probably dumped them in the woods, and then they had stumbled into a bulldozed trench used as the park dump. At first, we thought the moving things down there were rats, but then we climbed down and retrieved the full litter. By the end of the weekend, all the lucky puppies went home with new families. We named ours McCormick. Our other dogs were Brownie, Carmel, and Princess.

Princess was a climber. She climbed the steps on playground slides and slid down. She climbed the wooden ladders in the canyons of Turkey Run State Park; other hikers couldn't believe their eyes. She also climbed the six foot fence around the exercise yard at the vet, and escaped when we tried to board her there.

Brownie & Barbara

Carmel & Barb

We had our first cat when it adopted us in Bloomington Indiana, while Richard and I were still in college at Indiana University. That cat, Pug, was before even the biological children, and was enjoyed by fourteen years of children.

The next cat we had lived clandestinely upstairs with the children, and Richard and I were unaware of its existence! One teen had gone to a party with friends. The host family had a mother cat and kittens, but the mama cat was hit by a car, so the litter needed to be adopted.

Each person at the party won a kitten! This Burns prize was living in a dresser drawer upstairs. After about six weeks, the kitten found its way down 22 stairs to the living room, and came walking into the family room. Richard asked, "Where did that come from?" Barbara jumped up and took the kitten out the back door. What we didn't know was that she walked around the house and in the front door, taking the kitten back upstairs! All the kids knew it was living upstairs, but no one squealed, not even a kindergartener. Two weeks later, the same kitten came walking into the family room again, and this time Dad asked for a full explanation. I called the cat Seclusion, because she had lived in seclusion for so long.

We also had parakeets, hamsters, fish, and chipmunks. Once, our gerbils were about to enlarge their family, but we didn't know just when. Daughter Michele was in Italy on a class trip, and we went to pick her up from the Indianapolis Airport. Richard and I went to Indianapolis and the kids all stayed home. The plane was delayed by engine problems, and stopped in England, however, so after a long wait, we returned home without our traveler. We found all the kids at home crying, and trying to explain to us that the daddy gerbil was eating all the newborn babies! That was quite a science lesson with no adults around to help explain how a daddy gerbil would kill his offspring. Science 101: kids and animals are not predictable!

Marlene & Princess

Michele: One summer we had two twelve-month-old boys, unrelated, who were both on the verge of their first steps. We had a big black dog, Princess, whose mother was a registered collie, and whose father was a mutt who was very good at jumping fences.

Princess had long silky hair, and a maternal disposition. Those two baby boys tangled their sticky little fingers in her hair, and used it to pull themselves up to standing. She was their living "walker," and they would cruise with her as she walked slowly to keep from knocking them over. Once I came in and she looked up at me from the floor where she lay motionless, with a pleading look and tears in her eyes. One of the baby boys was teething on her ear, while the other was trampling her with the hard-soled little orthopedic shoes that were in vogue for toddlers in those days. Bless her heart; she would not disturb those babies. I took pity and plucked them off her.

Princess was a great addition to the care of all those kids. We did not train her to do this, but if a child was playing in our yard, and a male walked down the sidewalk, Princess would always discretely position herself between the child and the stranger. She did not make any noise and was never aggressive, but she stood and watched, and was ready.

On camping weekends, the children were not always with the adults. Several other families camped with us, so there were always multiple children exploring the trails and woodlands together. The children knew the trails, and the rules to be back at camp in time for meals. One weekend we had all but one daughter and another family's son, back at suppertime. We called out, but there was no answer. When they were an hour late we sent groups down the various trails, and supper was put on hold. The two missing kids were found on their knees, watching a snail that was wearing a harness made from thread. Michele had made it just as she had done before for little toads. The two were walking that snail home down the trail! No, we did not keep it as a pet. Yes, dinner was very late that night.

40 Sibling Groups, & Last Five Kids

Over time, we had quite a few two, three, or four-sibling groups. Our advantage was having five bedrooms, to make multiples possible. In later years, we knocked out a wall, making one downstairs bedroom part of the family room. We were naive to think we needed fewer bedrooms, but we really did need a larger family room. We thought our family would be smaller when our three daughters left home. We continued with foster placements, however, for thirty years.

Were visited by these three sweet sisters briefly

Two grandkids, with four foster siblings

Adorable brothers!

When I reached retirement age for teaching, I notified Welfare we were going to Florida for the winter, leaving in late October. We had five kids- three fifth grade girls, and two first grade boys.

In September, we were able to place one girl, Nancy, with her aunt in Kentucky. It took a truck to get her bike, clothes, and games all delivered. Today she is finishing her surgical nursing education and we are so very proud of her.

Dear Mom and Dad,

I want to take this time to tell you that I appreciate the time you took to raise me. I know that I was not the greatest person to raise, but you guys have never given up on me. I appreciate that we can still keep in touch, and no matter what is going on, I can still know you guys are Mom and Dad.

Some of my favorite memories are our travels to various places. I always think of our trip to Mackinac Island, Michigan. I loved our trip to Florida, and seeing Cape Canaveral. One of my most favorite memories is making bunny cakes at Easter time. I have always loved cooking and that is an awesome memory. I also liked holding the NASA moon rocks that you shared with us.

There are so many memories that I have with you and Dad. I wish things were different and I could come and visit you guys often, and enjoy some more time to make memories!

Love, Nancy

P.S. My graduation is July 28, 2016. I am graduating as a surgical technologist from Saint Louis Community College.

Four kids were left. A second girl went to the foster home she had been in before coming to us. That left one girl and two boys, a sibling group, and it was October. We loaded our camper for travel, and three weeks into October, the caseworker finally decided they would need to find a home, right then, for all three together. The three siblings were moved two days before we left the state, but then the biological parents showed up and protested the move. They didn't want the children moved from our house. We explained we were done with ice and snow; we were going south to our first warm retirement winter. The family realized we were going and acquiesced.

That foster daughter, Mollie, with the two little brothers, kept in touch with us. One day she called and announced that we could be proud of her and her husband. We knew they had a son, and wondered what the new news was. Her voice was bubbly and happy sounding, as she told us they were now foster parents, and would be getting their first placement that week! We really were proud of her. She didn't stay a foster parent very long. Her first placement was twin, newborn baby girls. After the first year, instead of fostering them, she decided to adopt them permanently! They are a beautiful addition to her family. The girls love their big brother, and the family travels and visits many historical places, museums, and parks! Success!

Marlene & Richard,

I remember how routine everything was at your house from the very first day. That was something very new to me. I remember riding my bike to school with Nancy and Inga, which was fun. I loved when you came home from school with lots of papers for us to help grade. Most of my memories probably involve us at home in the sunroom. That is where you taught me how to make a dream catcher. The sunroom is where I worked on my Hawaii project. I used your vacation pictures and videos to study. I had many firsts living with you. You took us to church regularly. I treasure our vacations at the campgrounds, and swimming in Lake Michigan. We got to go to summer camp at the YMCA. It was the first time I was in Girl Scouts, and our entire troop went to a sleepover in the Mounds Mall in Anderson, which was extremely exciting! I was not happy about having to move out. It was very difficult and sudden. We were placed in a home far away, with no contact with anyone we knew. We had to switch schools, and I was also not happy about that. Lol, I wish you lived closer so you could remind me how to make dream catchers for my own kids. You were an excellent teacher, with many talents. Your children are blessed to have such amazing parents. I'm blessed to have known you as well. Thank you for everything you have done for me, my brothers, and many other children.

Take care!

Mollie
(Summer 2016)

We built a large sunroom across the back of the house, and liked it so much we mostly lived out there.

41 Funding

Organizations and churches sometimes asked me to speak about our fostering experiences. My talk was never the same, as there were too many children and too many stories to cover. One topic that always came up, however, was our funding. After I finished talking I asked for questions. A hand went right up and the voice asked how much money I was paid, per child, because they knew we did it for the money. I explained we did get a stipend of $3.00 per day, which was $21 a week. If a child was a teenager, we only got $15 per week, because it was assumed teens would be doing dishes, and sweeping, or other housework, thereby earning their room and board. Our five pregnant teens, awaiting the births of their babies going for adoption, came under the $15 per week stipend. Actually, teens ate more, and needed more supplies, like pantyhose, lipstick, and tampons, so they cost more! Frequently we were told that the county funds were gone near the end of a month, and if siblings came into the system, we were asked to take two for the stipend of one, so we actually received a stipend of $1.50 per day! Sometimes I had to hire a babysitter, and my sitter got more for babysitting than I got for my stipend, while I had to provide shelter, food, clothes, and whatever other supplies the child needed, out of pocket.

After about 15 or so years into our fostering, the state held a foster parent conference. We met parents from all 92 Indiana counties and we talked! We learned that some counties paid a clothing allowance every month. Our county only had an initial clothing allowance of $25, and that was supposed to cover a coat, hat, and shoes. The rest of the wardrobe was out of pocket. Over time, after that conference, the initial clothing payment was raised to $50. A list was provided to us, of all necessary clothing items: shirts, jeans, underwear, sox, shoes, pajamas, coat, hat, mittens, raincoat, dresses, and sweatshirts. That took a big bite of funding. We learned that all the counties could set their stipends at any amount. We felt the state should have made all foster parents equal.

The woman who asked the question about funding, saying we took kids for the money, backed off with a quietly muttered, "Oh."

Ten years after we began fostering, the Madison County Welfare System reassessed boarding and clothing fees. The new amounts began in January of 1975. The Boarding fees changed from $3 per day to $4. They added 25 more cents if the child was between five and eleven. Ages twelve and up got 50 cents more. The initial clothing allowance was just that, initial, but they provided more funds for older children. The foster parents in counties with monthly clothing allowances didn't realize how lucky they were! I was reminded on the new rate letter that school books would be paid for the 9th grade pupils and up. Most of our kids were elementary and middle school, and even the elementary ages had very expensive (for us) book fees.

By 1995, when we retired after 30 years, the per diems averaged from ten dollars, to one special case, which was sixteen dollars. Most teenagers who babysit today would turn up their noses at such a fee for sitting. They charge an hourly rate! The funding letter was an eye-opening reminder of those earlier days. That lady who asked about funding in 1968 would still have probably said "Oh" in 1995, if she had a daughter who wanted to earn money babysitting!

MADISON COUNTY DEPARTMENT OF PUBLIC WELFARE CHILDREN

BOARDING RATES

BOARDING RATES EFFECTIVE 1-1-75:

AGES	AMOUNT (PER DIEM)	PLUS
Infant through age 5	$4.00	all medical and dental
Age 5 enrolled in kindergarten	$4.25	all medical and dental
Ages 6 through 11	$4.25	all medical and dental
Age 12 and up	$4.50	all medical and dental
Children with special needs	A rate not to exceed $5.00 per day may be established on a case-by-case basis.	

Change of per diem at first of the month preceding the birthday.

INITIAL CLOTHING ALLOWANCE FOR (one allowance only): NOT TO EXCEED

Infant through age 5	$30.00
Age 5 enrolled in kindergarten	$40.00
Ages 6 through 11	$40.00
Age 12 and up	$50.00

ALLOWANCE FOR SCHOOL BOOKS:

School books may be billed directly from the school to the Welfare Department for children who are enrolled in 9th grade and above.

MEDICAL AND DENTAL NEEDS:

Any medical or dental need up to $25.00 per month per child is automatically authorized by the department. A need over $25.00 per month must have prior authorization in writing from the department, with the exception of an emergency. A need exceeding $100.00 (except in an emergency) must have prior Board approval.

If a child has Medicaid eligibility under ADC-FC, the Medicaid card must be used rather than a direct billing to the Madison County Department of Public Welfare.

The above policy will be effective 1-1-75.

42 How the Child Protection System Works Today

Once there is a safe placement in shelter for children taken into state custody, a case manager sets up a shelter hearing so all parties involved know where the children are being sheltered. This can be with a fit and willing relative, someone who will take permanent guardianship, or a foster family. A dependency petition is filed by 21 days into the case. A week after that, an arraignment and shelter review is held. There is a "case plan" conference, which outlines steps, and the requirements the parents must meet to be reunited with their children. This conference is held with all involved with the case. Parents (even by phone from jail), the case manager, a Welfare lawyer, and the Guardian ad Litem for the child, or children, attend. The plan is printed and signed by all present. Each parent knows what he or she must do to get the family back together. Mom's plan often differs from Dad's plan. Welfare (Child Protective Services) keeps tabs on progress. The state may require blood tests, employment reports, housing reports, or whatever else the case plan stipulates. If visitation is allowed, that is a major item for consideration. Do parents make visits, are they on time, and are the visits good for the child?

During the next six months, the foster parents and GAL are the main people who see the children. The case managers see the child occasionally, but the lawyers and judges never do.

At court, the reports from the foster parents and GAL are the hands-on information the judge considers. The reports made regularly to the case managers are in the written reports the judge receives. (I like to include photos in my reports, as it lets the judge see the actual child, on whose behalf he or she will make decisions).

At twelve months into a case, a Judicial Permanency Review is held, to see if the case plans are being met. All along that time line there are status reviews, so all involved are aware of any shortcomings, and there are services offered to help get the parents on track for reunification. Putting children back into a family situation that was seriously dysfunctional, is a weighty decision. Sometimes medical care is needed. Counseling is needed. Tutoring is needed. All is provided while a child is in foster care.

When Richard and I first began fostering, there were none of the above information sharing opportunities set up. I did go to judicial hearings to testify about my children. We didn't know about any of the work by Welfare on behalf of the children. We knew things happened, and they came to collect our kids whenever the parents met all the requirements. The longer we had a child, the less hopeful we were about a successful return to biological parents. When our son Larry was still with us, after arriving just after kindergarten and staying all the way to eighth grade, I decided to take things into my own hands. I wrote to the governor and representatives about giving legal freedom to Larry and his sister. The governor pardons criminals at the end of each December, so I thought he could consider giving these children a pardon and release them from legal limbo, to be adopted by a permanent family. The kids had served seven and a half years in foster care, and the parental rights were still not terminated. I knew of a family that wanted to adopt both children, so adoption would take place as soon as the home evaluations were complete. The potential mom was a schoolteacher, and her husband was an optician. They had no children.

Then I had a phone call from my Welfare case manager, Nellie, asking, “Marlene, what have you done?” She said the governor had called her boss, who was very surprised! While it didn't work to free the children, it did call attention to the fact that the case was a very old case. The court finally did declare parental rights terminated, and both children did get the security of permanent lives with the parents who had cared for them for most of their lives! Larry tried a short placement with another family, but came back to us and kept his name. He didn't want to be adopted, but wanted to stay right where he was and keep his name, and a permanent family.

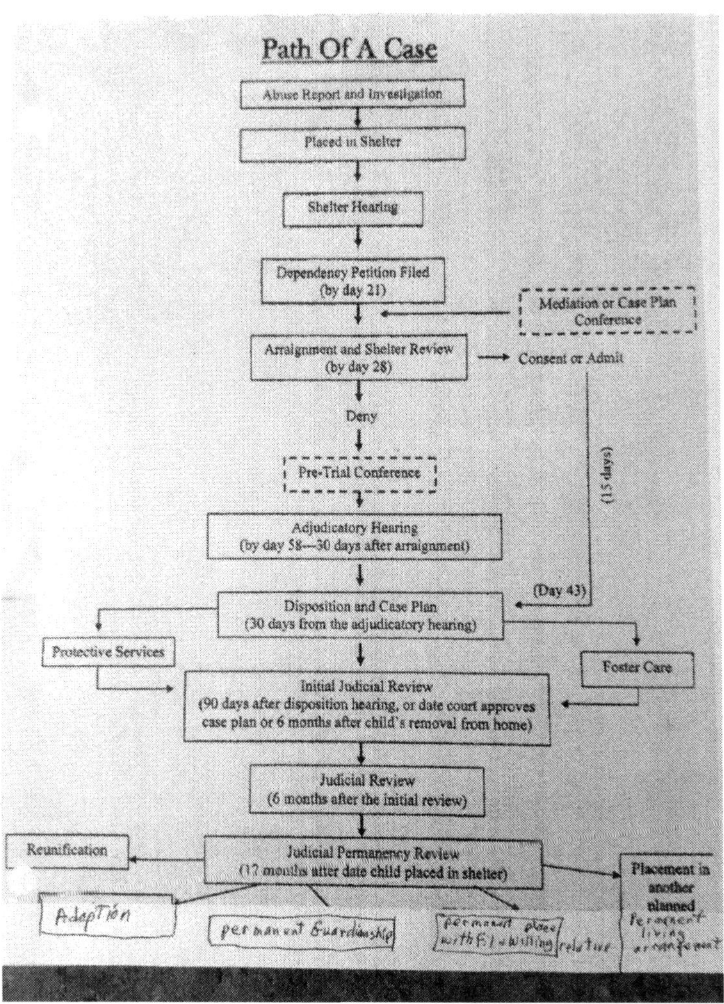
Path Of A Case
Abuse Report and Investigation
Placed in Shelter
Shelter Hearing
Dependency Petition Filed
(by day 21)
Mediation or Case Plan
Conference
Arraignment and Shelter Review
(by day 28)
Consent or Admit
Deny
Pre-Trial Conference
(15 days)
Adjudicatory Hearing
(by day 58—30 days after arraignment)
(Day 43)
Disposition and Case Plan
(30 days from the adjudicatory hearing)
Protective Services
Foster Care
Initial Judicial Review
(90 days after disposition hearing, or date court approves
case plan or 6 months after child's removal from home)
Judicial Review
(6 months after the initial review)
Reunification
Judicial Permanency Review
(12 months after date child placed in shelter)
Placement in
another
planned
Adoption
permanent Guardianship

43 Travel Entertainment, Etc.

Richard and I were often asked how we kept so many kids occupied and happy on long trips. He had a pat answer: "Oh, she always teaches all the way out and all the way back."

Every trip is an adventure for us, and we try to make them an adventure for each child. Some of the games we used in the car were no-storage and no-little-pieces types.

- Spot license plates from every state, each person has to do their own collection—no partners.
- ABCs. Find consecutive letters of alphabet on signs along the highway. (Another must also see it, to verify.)
- Counting horses. All, or a particular color. Out west, it was pretty easy to get a good count!
- Slug a Bug. Find Volkswagen Beatles; preschoolers could excel at this.
- Bingo Travel cards with sliding covers for items on the card, a nice quiet game.
- Sing songs- some the kids know, and some I teach them
- Learning road signs, shapes and words. One girl asked what mer-ga was, and I was stumped. I asked where she saw it. She showed me a road sign- "merge." It is a funny memory still.

- Write post cards. All the kids had to write post cards to their parents from sites visited.
- Oral math games. Add, subtract, or multiply, depending on ages. We also did basic facts in Spanish: uno y uno son dos, cinco menos dos son tres.
- Contests. Pay a quarter to the first person who spots something we know is ahead of us. For example, the St. Louis Arch, which is visible a long time before you get to it.

I also find it handy to keep a roll of paper towels, a plastic peanut butter jar filled with soapy water, and trash bags in the car.

I used shower organizers on the backs of car seats for storage—pencils, small books, flip-flops.

I find it best to keep most eating outside the vehicle, if possible; that saves a lot of cleanup.

44 Coordinating Family and Work

Coordinating a full time teaching job, and having three to eight children at home, isn't easy. Getting a second college degree while managing a full time teaching job, kids, and a nine room house, is also not easy, but all of these at the same time might seem like mission impossible! I did it with Richard's help. Once I had my bachelor's degree, I went right into teaching a second grade class of forty-two students. I thought I would never finish grading all those workbooks!

After I began teaching, Indiana changed the requirement for teacher licensing, requiring a master's degree, so I did night classes and summer sessions, driving from Elwood to Muncie, for four years. I carried as many as twenty-two credit hours at a time (most students average fifteen.) I figured I had to do as much as possible while on campus. One art professor offended me by reporting me absent three times. I had never missed class. I questioned why he did that and was told that everyone cuts a few times, so he just reports cuts for everyone. I spent my money for the class, my gas to get there, and I definitely wanted credit for all I was achieving. I felt betrayed and lied about. I vowed to always make my student reports accurate.

I carpooled with other mothers doing what I was doing. We tried to get classes scheduled as near alike as possible. We all had kids at home and meals to fix. My babysitter accepted baked goods for payment, and after she got my recipes, she learned to bake for herself. One year she cleaned my house for my birthday, which was a perfect present. I never had outside help with any cleaning, laundry or cooking. Organization played a big part of managing everything in mere 24 hour days. Richard was always my helping hand.

How did I manage my college homework? I did most all my reading in the bathtub!

When we remodeled the bathroom, I had Richard install a light above the tub. There were sliding glass doors on the tub making a "reading area," but the toilet was still available if needed. If I tried reading anywhere else, someone was always asking for something, but my reading tub was off limits.

The reading room

Richard had been working at a furniture store (Taff & Baker) two blocks from our house. Once I began teaching, however, he changed jobs and worked for Western Electric. He had to work out of town, sometimes for a month. He was sent to Columbus Ohio, Nashville Tennessee, and Michigan City Indiana. He only got to be home on weekends. I notified Welfare that he was gone, because I figured they wanted a two-parent family for the foster kids. They explained their children needed to see that a daddy could leave for work, but would always come home and support his family. I learned how it felt to be a single parent, and I missed his support! The county kept all the foster kids with us in our changed family situation.

45 Closet that Talks

You have probably heard the expression, "If these walls could talk!" Well, we had a bedroom upstairs with a walk-in closet, and those walls did talk. The closet was wallpapered in light green paper with flowers on it, circa 1930. When we took all the wallpaper out of that bedroom, we left the closet alone, as it still looked pretty. Later, when we painted the bedroom each time, we considered painting the closet, but its walls had changed! Children autographed it. They wrote poems on it. They drew pictures on it and wrote thank you letters for letting them live there. After a child was gone for some time, they would sometimes return, and the first thing they wanted to do was go up to that closet and show their spouse or friend what they had contributed to the walls. It was well-decorated, and when we put the house up for sale after living there 54 years, we cleaned out the closet. We left the closet walls as they were during the showings, but we had a letter posted on the outside of the door. It stated that over 30 years 103 children had lived upstairs, and this was their artwork, and heart felt love was in that room. Even if a child came back more than once, they still had to go see that closet! It had the look of early pictoglyphs. Once the whole house was empty, we took photos of the letters and art, the autographs and poems. Then the wallpaper was scraped off and the room was painted. I saved a foot square of paper, with one particular letter telling us how much it meant to the girl who lived in that room, and how she felt safe and would always remember her time with our family. She said it was the best place she had ever lived.

46 Jury Duty

There have been two situations I experienced that involved children, but not foster children. I was Involved with the lives of a victim of rape, and a perpetrator of murder and theft. The perpetrator was a seventeen-year-old boy who was part of a teenage gang. The gang put crime names on cards and put them in a can. For fun, they pulled out a card each week and did whatever the card said. They had pulled out arson and burned the Anderson Hotel to the ground.

My involvement involved being sequestered with a jury of sixteen, to deliberate the charges mentioned above. We lived in a hotel for over three weeks. Richard was able to visit me for an hour each Sunday afternoon. The jury was bussed to various restaurants, so no one knew just where we were. We had guards at all times, even when we did laundry down the hall of the hotel!

The seventeen-year-old and his friends had murdered a sixty-year-old woman, and had taken $11.17 from her; it was all she had. They were mad at finding so little money, and stabbed her mercilessly. They took the money and went to a movie. After the movie they went back to the apartment and found she was still alive, and beat her until she was dead. Our jury found this seventeen-year-old guilty, and he was given the death penalty. He is still on death row after twenty-nine years.

I believe I was selected for that jury because of my foster parenting. The boy was bullied and sickly, with runny eyes. He is an example of a child that both family and the system failed. He used the crime club to feel strong. My dealings with many children made me a candidate to listen and act regarding a teenage perpetrator.

The rape victim was a six-year-old girl. She was so torn and injured that she needed surgical repairs. She appeared in court and testified about her situation, and pointed to her mom's boyfriend as her rapist. The prosecutor showed her a Vaseline jar and asked her to read it, but she didn't know the words. He asked if she had seen the jar before, and what was it used for. She testified the boyfriend used it so he wouldn't hurt her so much. He made her do a pinky promise not to tell her mother.

Again, I felt I was chosen to be on that jury because I was a foster parent. The other jurors made me the foreman of this jury. This perpetrator was sentenced to life in prison for raping a child under the age of twelve.

In both cases, a jury decided the future of a child. One for committing a crime, is still waiting for his sentence to be carried out. The other has healed physically, but will always remember her trauma. I was charged with the task of participating in those life-altering decisions, as you may one day be, if called. Many people try to avoid jury duty, but it is an element of citizenship, and an integral part of our justice system. It is a sort of sacred trust to participate in influencing justice, and your fellow citizen's lives in the United States.

47 Guardian ad Litem

In 2009, the Okeechobee News had an ad for Guardian ad Litem (GAL) volunteers. A GAL visits children in the foster system, collects information, and speaks for the children in court. Richard told me to sign up. He said I'd had more children than most volunteers that might sign up, so I volunteered from 2009 through 2016. I have represented six girls, seven boys, and four courtesy cases (children from other counties who live in Okeechobee County.) Four of my kids have been adopted, and there are three siblings in the adoption process now. I just got four new children.

I go to the 19th Circuit Court in Okeechobee for all my children's hearings. I also went to the Belle Glade court in Palm Beach County for two of my boys. That day I had a bonus for my time, as there are beautiful glass mural panels depicting plants, animals and birds in South Florida. My photos that day had little boys, and a striking mural.

My GAL boss covers over a hundred children. There is an average of twenty volunteers to help with those children. It seems the need for volunteers is greater than what the recruiters can produce! As my three siblings went into the adoption process, my boss acquired seven new family cases.

Richard and I took care of children for 30 years, and through the GAL system I have represented twenty-four more, (but they were not eating and sleeping with us!) I just can't seem to avoid having a finger in children's lives.

48 AmeriCorps

In the 2013/14 school year, another ad in the Okeechobee News asked for AmeriCorps reading-teacher volunteers for a local elementary school. The ad begged for help. I turned in my resume and knew they wouldn't choose me, because I am too old. But, oh yes they did! I taught one more year of elementary reading, after being retired for eighteen years! I felt like I had never been out of the classroom. I loved the kids and they worked hard for me.

One brother and sister made my year very special. They had moved to Florida from a southern state. The ten-year-old boy was placed in 4th grade, but did not yet know the alphabet. The girl was placed in 3rd. She did know the alphabet, but had a limited reading vocabulary. This challenge was one I had never met in my thirty years of teaching. The lessons began with pre-K level materials. By October, the boy had learned to read nineteen words on his hundred-word list. He hugged me that day and said, "Mrs. Burns, I never knew I could learn so many words!" Other teachers would walk by and mouth to me, "Is he reading?" I smiled and nodded my head yes! He was up to 100 words by Christmas, 200 by February, and 400 by April. Best of all was the fact that he knew he could read, and all books could be in his future. His sister was nearly at grade level by year-end.

No matter how I have been in contact with children: by birth, our fosters, my classroom, Church school, AmeriCorps readers, and Guardian ad Litem, they all have impacted my life, and thereby have impacted Richard. We had a great introduction to a world with many little feet, and every bit of it has been worth it.

49 Young-Marrieds to Great-Grandparents

When young couples marry, they have no way of knowing how their lives will evolve. How many kids will there be, or where they will live may be a mystery. There is no guarantee as to what type of job they will have. Changes occur, and there are happy times and sad times. We grow by what happens, and if you let your partner support you in woeful times, you can both celebrate in the wonderful times.

Richard and I had to live through the sad times, but we survived stronger and more positive to be able to enjoy every one of our 103 children. We believe the children in our lives have kept us young. I was 58 and Richard was 66 when we had our last five foster children, before we left for Florida. We were parenting a family as a twenty or thirty-something would do in a typical family.

We kept healthy, and the children kept us active. We rode bikes all those years, up and down the streets and roads of Madison County. Richard was usually the leader, and I brought up the rear, with a train of bikes in between. Sometimes two or three, but as many as six or eight were in the middle. One baby who rode in the carrier of my bike always rode with her feet in the middle of my back, or Richard's if he was the driver. Her legs reached just that far, so she always propped them up.

We moved to Florida in 1995 and we thought our days of extra children had ended. Then a family moved into the empty house next door, with a four-year-old boy and a six-year-old girl. *Of course,* we became grandparents to them. We kept the girl the night her new baby sister was born, and that added a third grandchild, Florida style. Children just become attached to us, and we have been parents for 59 of our 61 years of marriage. Our *Mom* and *Dad* names have been used by every child. As new children joined our family, they used the labels of the original kids. The new generations automatically say grandma and grandpa. Our biological great-grands say Grandpa Great and Grandma Great, after one grandchild, Casey, charmingly mislabeled my mother, Grandma Great, instead of great-grandma. It was apt, so we never corrected her and it became a tradition. There was one exception: one three-year-old called me Gramma Grape!

50 Richard

Richard says that every child we have encountered in the last fifty years has been an entertaining challenge. At no time have we ever failed completely, but we came close a few times. We have been lucky to better the lives of most of them. Some we rescued from terrible situations. They, in return, rescued us from a life of mediocrity. He says thank you to you all, for sharing your lives with us.

Michele here: The foster care system is proof to me that some people should not have kids. There is no better advertisement for free universal access to birth control. Often parents have good intentions, but fail as parents due to various impediments. As a society we must address this reality and help failing parents with drug and alcohol treatment, or mental health care, or whatever it takes, but we must also ensure a loving safety net for the children; there simply are no "throw away people."

We all are implicated and impacted when we fail children. Society, therefore, has an obligation to invest what it takes to intervene and shepherd abused or neglected children toward functional, joyful lives- so far as we can. What I gleaned from living with foster kids was that the orphanage was like a children's prison, and training facility for future criminals. Kids there were taught by other kids, how to survive without caring adults. They learned how to run, how to steal, how to sell their bodies to stay alive. We can and must do better for our precious children.

Too few people step up to take in these stranded kids, most of whom live in legal limbo- not free to be adopted, but not able to return to parents. Many foster kids have emotional wounds and need extra love and care, which institutions may not be able to provide. These kids are also amazingly resilient, and capable of being loving, happy, and well-adjusted, given a healthy environment; the "difficult cases" are the minority.

States are desperate for foster families, and most state programs are shamefully understaffed and underfunded. I know my own children are the best things in my life, and the hardest. Don't have any illusions that it is easy, but do remember that we are creatures who need connection; without it life has no meaning. If you have the emotional and material resources, please consider opening your home and your heart to a foster child.

If you are a legislator or other official with the power to enable better funding of foster care and child protection systems, please make that happen!

If you are an ordinary citizen, please spur your representatives in government to include adequate funding for the children in your state.

FOR SALE
BY OWNER

Appendix

For more information on foster care, I recommend Mallory Duncan's excellent 2015 documentary, titled *Barriers*. It is available on Vimeo, and examines the foster care system in Indiana from various angles, including sections on misconceptions, neglect, mistrust, and the politics involved.

A statistic from Duncan's documentary that I found interesting is that there were (in 2015) over 17,000 children in the Indiana foster care system.

The film cites the neglect on the part of the Department of Child Services (DCS) that occurred due to severe overload of case managers. Extreme shortage of staff, Duncan explains, can limit case managers to "putting out fires," and this leads to harms for vulnerable children.

https://blogs.butler.edu/multimedia-journalism/2015/05/03/barriers-documentary-indiana-foster-care-system/

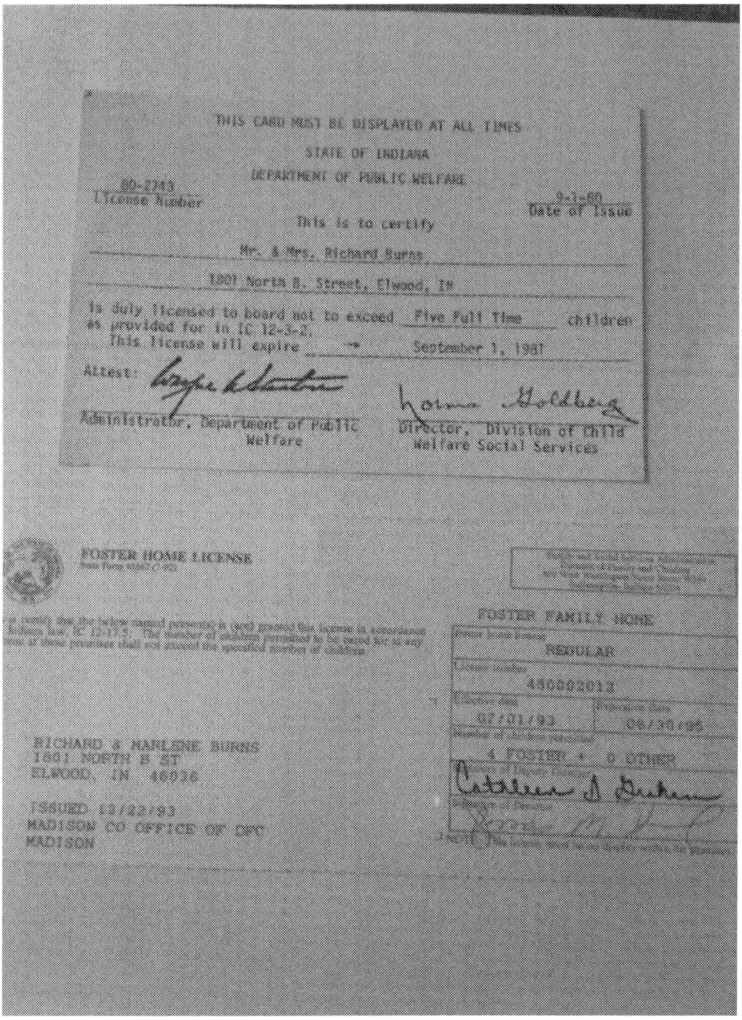

THIS CARD MUST BE DISPLAYED AT ALL TIMES

STATE OF INDIANA

DEPARTMENT OF PUBLIC WELFARE

80-2743
License Number

9-1-80
Date of Issue

This is to certify

Mr. & Mrs. Richard Burns

1801 North B. Street, Elwood, IN

is duly licensed to board not to exceed Five Full Time children as provided for in IC 12-3-2.
This license will expire → September 1, 1981

Attest:

Administrator, Department of Public Welfare

Director, Division of Child Welfare Social Services

FOSTER HOME LICENSE

FOSTER FAMILY HOME

REGULAR

480002012

07/01/93

06/30/95

4 FOSTER + 0 OTHER

RICHARD & MARLENE BURNS
1801 NORTH B ST
ELWOOD, IN 46036

ISSUED 12/22/93
MADISON CO OFFICE OF DFC
MADISON

Certificate of Recognition

This Certifies That

Richard and Marlene Burns

Has attained special honor for excellence in

Foster Care for 21 years

And is hereby awarded this certificate by

Madison Co. Dept. of Public Welfare

Organization

Anderson, Indiana

City and State

on this twelfth day of September 19 87

[illegible], Supervisor [illegible], Director

OFFICE OF THE GOVERNOR

INDIANAPOLIS, INDIANA 46204

ROBERT D. ORR
GOVERNOR

February 2, 1981

Mrs. Marlene Burns
1801 North "B" Street
Elwood, Indiana 46036

Dear Mrs. Burns:

Under Indiana law the local court is responsible for determining custody of children. The court has ordered Larry placed in foster care. The Madison County Department of Public Welfare is working with Larry and his mother in an attempt to reunite the family. Should this plan prove unsuccessful, the county department will take whatever action is necessary and in Larry's best interest.

Your efforts in caring for Larry and his sister Cheryl are deeply appreciated. Please be encouraged to continue working with the Madison County Department of Public Welfare in planning for the children's future. If you continue to have concerns about their situation, please discuss these with Mr. Clifford Bennett, Director, Madison County Department of Public Welfare, 16 East Ninth Street, Anderson 46015.

Sincerely,

ROBERT D. ORR
Governor

RDO:sr

The attempt to get Larry out of "legal limbo" called for some agitating.

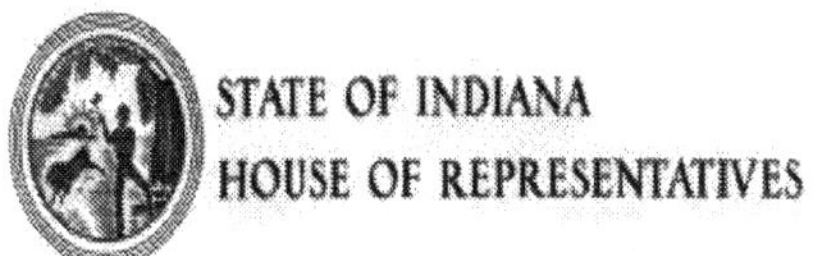

STATE OF INDIANA
HOUSE OF REPRESENTATIVES

RICHARD M. DELLINGER
MAJORITY LEADER
THIRD FLOOR STATE HOUSE
INDIANAPOLIS, INDIANA 46204

January 23, 1981

Mrs. Marlene Burns
1801 North B
Elwood, Indiana 46036

Dear Mrs. Burns:

Thank you for providing me a copy of your letter to Governor Orr and former Governor Bowen, concerning adoption procedures and the problem you have encountered in attempting to help Larry. You are to be commended for your efforts to help children in need of a sound family setting.

For your information, the legislature has been looking at the adoption process through interim study committees. While no substantial legislative changes have been made, I do anticipate further review of the matter that may result in possible legislative action. You may be assured that I will watch for any proposal that attempts to improve the adoption process. However, until some changes are enacted, it appears that your only remedy is to continue to pursue the matter according to existing procedures.

Again, thank you for writing.

Sincerely,

Dick Dellinger

Richard M. Dellinger
Majority Leader

RMD/cf

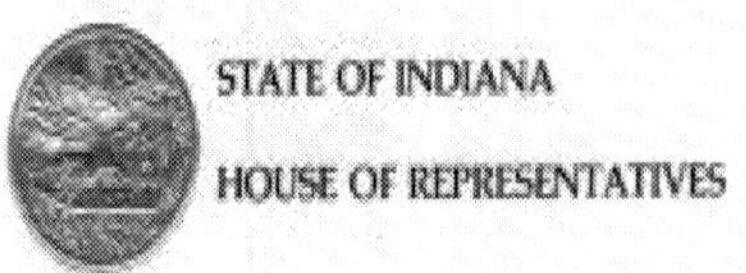

STATE OF INDIANA

HOUSE OF REPRESENTATIVES

Richard O. Regnier

Committees:

Cities & Towns, Ranking Member

Elections & Apportionment

February 3, 1981

Mrs. Marlene Burns
1801 North "B" Street
Elwood, Indiana 46036

Dear Mrs. Burns:

Thank you for your letter of January 12, 1981 regarding Larry and his sister. As a lawyer by trade, I've experienced similar disappointments in the court room in the past three years. At this point, I'm not sure what it takes to shock the conscience of some of my brethern who occupy our benches. We have virtually taken our courts and their probation departments out of politics in order to shield them from some of the social pressures of our communities and give them more freedom to make fair and just decisions. However, it still takes a strong judge who has the backbone to look squarely at a parent like Larry's mother and say "this is wrong" and "we are primarily interested in your children because you have goofed your opportunity to be a responsible parent."

My only suggestion is the possibility of having child abuse charges brought against the mother with the support of the Madison County Probation Department with a request that the children be made wards of the court for eventual placement for adoption. Because all these matters are governed by law and by the decisions of our courts, your only recourse is legal assistance and more litigation. Even then, under our present hands off attitude toward "moral" wrongs exhibited by our courts. I'd say your chances are less than 50-50. Good luck and don't give up.

Sincerely,

Richard O. Regnier
State Representative
District 27

ROR/bb

The Bronnenberg Children's Home, Anderson Indiana
(demolished, and replaced with cabins in the 1980s)
Photo credit Norm Cook

Marlene Herr Burns was born in Ladysmith, Wisconsin. She grew up and was educated in Gary, Indiana. She went to Lew Wallace High School, and later Indiana University, where she met future husband, Richard Burns. She received Bachelor of Science, and Master of Arts degrees from Ball State University. In 1985, she was a candidate for Teacher in Space, and used the NASA research materials to enrich her classroom. Science and history were her favorite subjects during the thirty years she taught elementary school in Elwood and Tipton Indiana.

In 1988, she joined teachers from around the state at the Indiana Junior Historical Society Summer History Camps and Teacher Workshops. The living history at the camps led to her creation of a first-person character, Sheshebens, a Native American fur trader.

Marlene performs as Sheshebens at schools, libraries, churches, and other venues, to teach about the Hoosier fur-trading era. She received the Indiana Council for Social Studies Distinguished Teacher Award, and the Outstanding Elementary Geography Teacher of the Year Award. She retired from teaching in 1995.

Marlene and Richard now live in Okeechobee Florida, where she is a Guardian ad Litem for the 19th Circuit Court. She has been an AmeriCorps volunteer reading teacher in Okeechobee, and is a member of the Okeechobee Community Choir. Marlene and Richard belong to the Okeechobee Presbyterian Church, where she sings in the choir, and is a deacon.

Reading, stitching, cooking, and painting eggs and various other objects, are Marlene's current hobbies.

Made in the USA
Middletown, DE
18 December 2016